UEFA

euro96 England

The Official Book

THIS IS A CARLTON BOOK

This edition published in 1996

10 9 8 7 6 5 4 3 2

A CIP catalogue record for this book is available from the British Library

ISBN 0 09 181407 3

Project Editor: Martin Corteel

Project art direction: Paul Messam

Production: Sarah Schuman

Picture research: Sharon Hutton

Designed by Jon Lucas

Editorial Assistant: David Ballheimer

Printed and bound in Great Britain

PICTURE ACKNOWLEDGEMENTS

The publishers would like to thank the following sources for their kind permission to reproduce the images in this book: **Action Images**; **Allsport**/Shaun Botterill, Clive Brunskill, Simon Bruty, David Cannon, Michael Cooper, Mike Hewitt, Hulton Deutsch, Ross Kinnaird, Gary M Prior, Ben Radford, Dave Rogers, Mark Thompson, Vandystadt; **Associated Press**; **Colorsport**/Temp/Liewig; **Empics**/Morton, Neal Simpson; **Images**; **Popperfoto**/D. Joyner, Reuters, SAG. Additional thanks go to **Chorley Hanford Limited/Premier Image** (Unit 12, 157–159 Boundfield Road, London SE6 1PE, England)

(CAPTION PAGE 5, TOP TO BOTTOM) **EURO96™ CONTENDERS** ***England, France, Croatia, Russia, Portugal, Denmark, Holland, Spain***

THE OFFICIAL BOOK

KEIR RADNEDGE

CARLTON

OFFICIAL SPONSORS

McDonald's

CONTENTS

Two faces of England Inset: ***English soccer fans in good cheer;*** Main picture: ***the Tower of London, one of the most famous landmarks in the capital***

INTRODUCTION

"Football comes home" ... the slogan for Euro96™ says everything about the finals of 1996 European Championship.

It reflects England's historical role in the development of association football, but also the impatience generated by the 36 years it has taken to bring Europe's most important national team event to the birthplace of the organized game.

The excitement raised by the prospect of seeing the finest 16 nations from the length and breadth of Europe meant that, more than a year before the kick-off, on June 8, almost £11 million had already been spent by fans snapping up the first 300,000 of the 1.4 million tickets.

English football is ideally equipped to host Euro96™. The redevelopment of the country's top stadia meant all-seater grounds were ready and waiting. The most sophisticated security arrangements have been put in place – and the television and general media coverage will be second to none.

Euro96™ is the most important sports event to be staged in England since the 1966 World Cup. Yet, in terms of global coverage and worldwide interest, it will reach even more homes and football fans than events of 30 years ago.

The presence of superstar players such as England's Alan Shearer, Germany's Jürgen Klinsmann, Italy's Paolo Maldini and Bulgaria's Hristo Stoichkov promises to make this one of the most memorable football events of modern times ... anywhere.

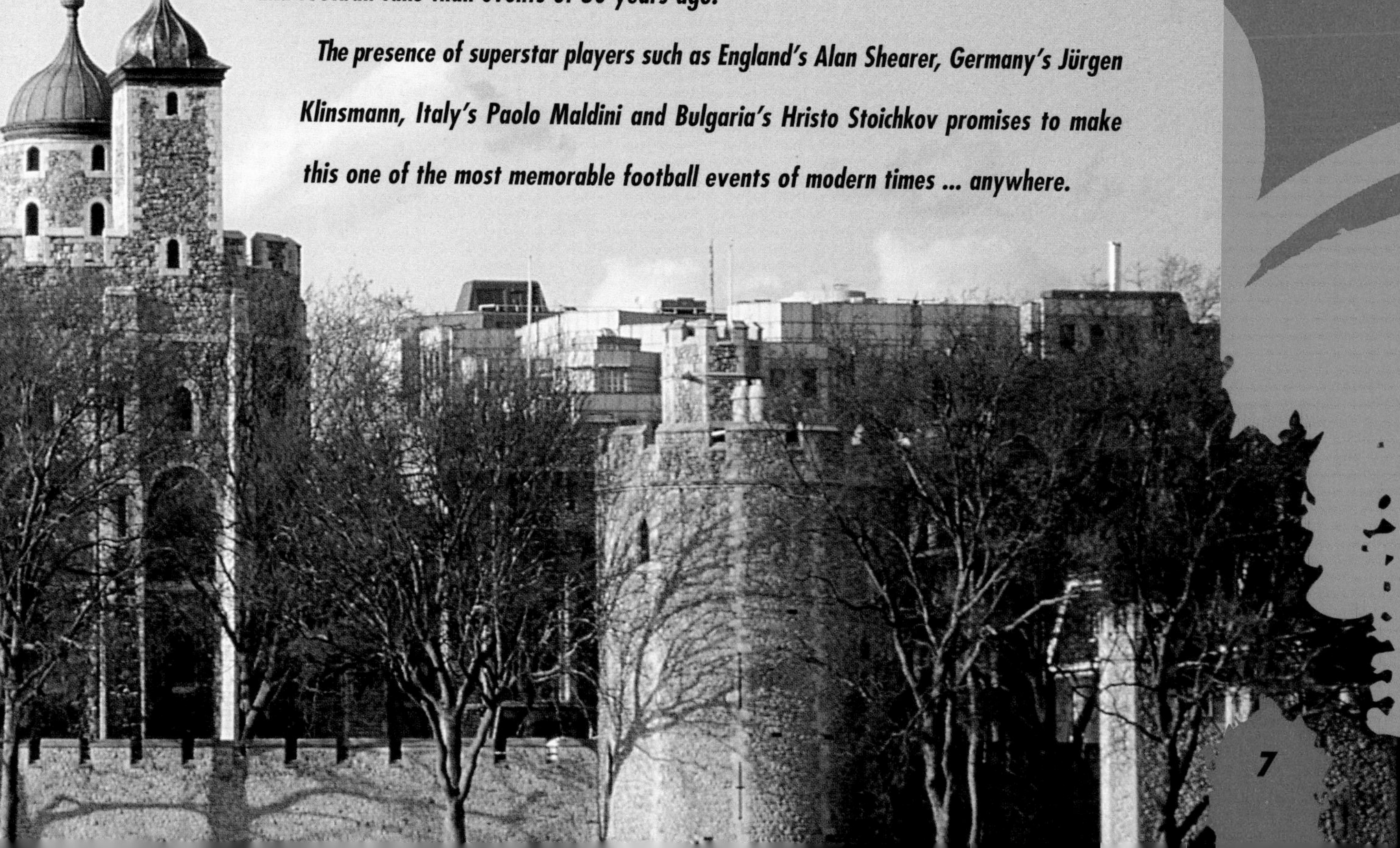

The 1996 European Championship Finals

The finals of the 1996 European Championship open at Wembley Stadium on Saturday, June 8 – when hosts England kick off the tournament against Switzerland – and end on the same stage on Sunday, June 30. Yet although England have yet to kick a ball in competitive pursuit of the 1996 European Championship, their preparation began earlier than any of the other 15 nations.

January 1991 was the date when the Football Association decided to seek hosting rights. The formal bid was delivered to UEFA in November 1991 and approved on May 6, 1992.

Interestingly, it was not until the following November that UEFA confirmed speculation and doubled the size of the finals from eight to 16 nations. Since all interested candidates had been asked to submit proposals for hosting an event of either size, the FA had no problem stepping up the scope of the event. Indeed, the tournament organizers would have been confronted with a serious embarrassment of riches had the event been restricted to eight nations.

As Ernie Walker, chairman of UEFA's stadia commission, said after a visit to one of the sites: "City for city, England has the best football stadia in the world." Walker had led a five-strong delegation from the European governing body on an inspection tour of the likely venues. Careful attention was paid to the seating arrangements for fans and media. Around 250,000 foreign visitors are expected to flood into England for the finals while more than 1,000 media representatives are likely to attend any one game.

The draw for the finals duly went ahead at the International Convention Centre in Birmingham on Sunday, December 17, at which the 16 nations were split into four groups of four. England the hosts, Denmark the holders and Spain and Germany, based on their qualifying records in the 1994 World Cup and 1996 European Championship, were the four seeds kept apart.

National Lottery

The draw provided England with Switzerland as opponents in the Opening Match at Wembley on June 8. Altogether the 31 matches of the finals will be watched by a cumulative television audience around the world of almost 7 billion.

Organizing Euro96™ on behalf of the Football Association is Glen Kirton, the Tournament Director. Beneath him is a staffing pyramid which includes full-time officials and – when it comes to the finals themselves – a 1,000-strong army of volunteers. They will be put to work in all the various support roles including acting as interpreters, liaison officers, drivers and media aides.

Just the Ticket

The ticketing system for fans was designed to provide as much flexibility as possible for visiting nations while retaining security standards.

The sales system was designed to reward loyalty, with domestic tickets first having been offered to the England "football family" and then to the public in general. Tickets were sold on an individual basis with a maximum of four tickets per match per person. Any fan who wanted to apply for tickets for the knock-out stages had to apply for group matches as well. Any remaining single tickets were expected to be put on general sale from May 1, 1996.

No expense has been spared to make Euro96™ an ideal advertisement for football in general and English football in particular.

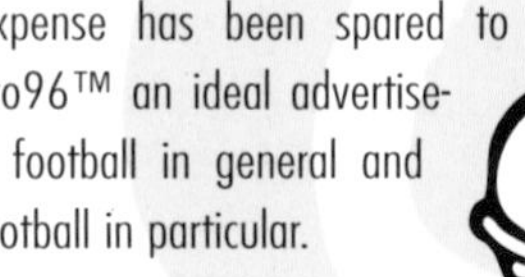

EURO FACT *The official mascot of the 1996 European Championship is Goaliath – developed by The Football Association to reflect all the fun and enthusiasm which the tournament will generate. Older England fans, with long memories and an eye for a happy coincidence, may consider that Goaliath bears more than a passing resemblance to World Cup Willy.*

Big ticket *England coach Terry Venables shows off a Euro96™ Final ticket but he hopes his seat will be by the pitch*

"We can stage a memorable tournament, a colourful tournament, efficiently run, enjoyable, safe and secure. We know that the expectations of a tournament in England will be high and we are confident we can match those expectations. We want the game's homecoming to be a happy one."

Glen Kirton, Euro96™ Tournament Director.

Preparing the Way

THE VENUES

The Stately Football Homes of England

England is ideally equipped to host major international football events. It boasts probably the finest collection of soccer-specific stadia in Europe, if not the world. Naturally enough, the finals open and close at Wembley – the site of the 1966 World Cup Final – one the world's most famous football grounds and fabled "Venue of Legends". Here is a look at the eight venues.

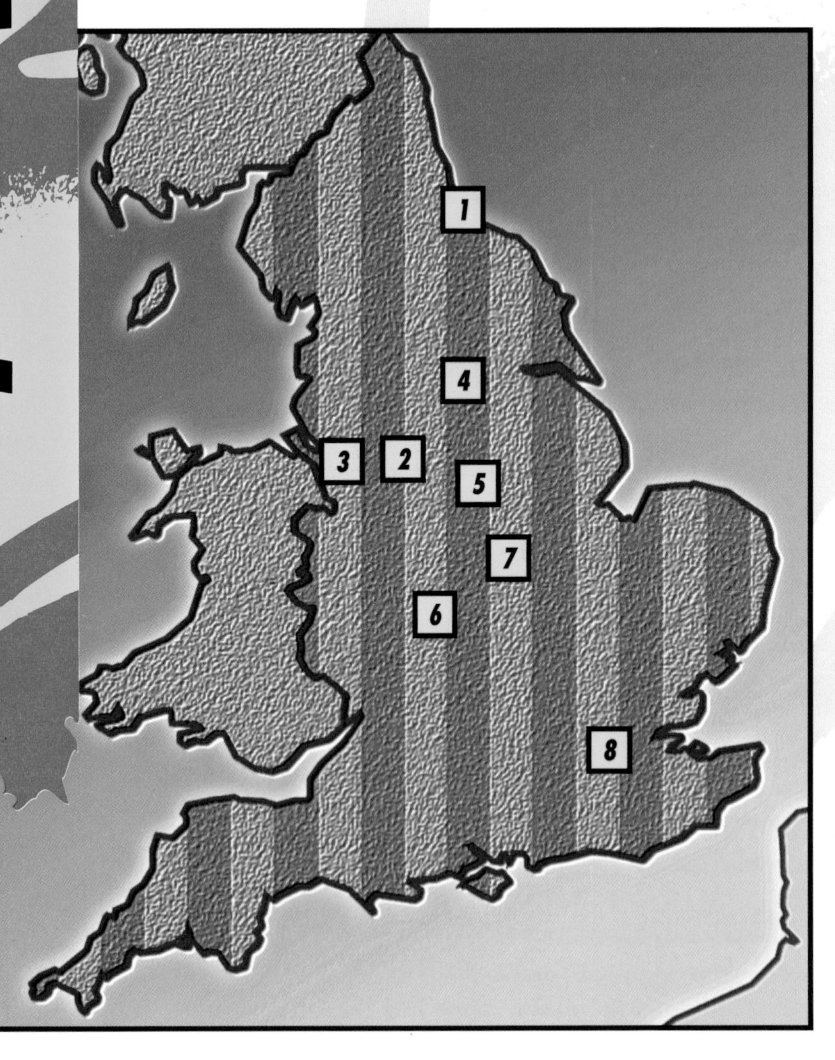

ST JAMES' PARK, Newcastle-Upon-Tyne

Description: The site of St James' Park has been the home of Newcastle United since 1892. In 1953, it became only the third First Division ground in England to be equipped with floodlights. The ground is home to one ofthe most passionate groups of fans in English football, who like to congregate at the Gallowgate end.
Host club: Newcastle United are four-times English league champions, six-times winners of the FA Cup and winners of the UEFA Cup in 1978. In the late 1980s and early 1990s the club teetered on the brink of bankruptcy, but the arrival of Kevin Keegan as manager returned the club to their position of glamour.
Capacity: 35,000
Pitch measurements: 110 yd x 73 yd (101m x 67m)

HILLSBOROUGH, Sheffield

Description: Hillsborough, in the Owlerton suburb of Sheffield in South Yorkshire, opened in 1899. One of football's major tragedies occurred at Hillsborough, when 95 fans died in 1989. Extensive redevelopment has since taken place to ensure it is one of the safest sports arenas in the country.
Host club: Host club are Sheffield Wednesday, the fifth oldest League club, having been founded in 1867. Wednesday have won the League four times, the FA Cup three times and the Football League Cup once. In 1993, they lost in both the FA Cup and League Finals.
Capacity: 40,000
Pitch measurements: 115 yd x 77 yd (105m x 70m)

> ***"Wembley is the cathedral of football ... the home of the beautiful game."***
>
> *Pelé, football's legendary ambassador.*

OLD TRAFFORD, Manchester

2

Description: Old Trafford has been the home of Manchester United since 1910, and regularly housed crowds more than 60,000. In 1996, another tier was added to raise the capacity to over 50,000.
Host club: Manchester United won the FA Carling Premiership in consecutive seasons, 1992–93 and 1993–94, on the second occasion claiming a double with FA Cup success. In 1968, Manchester United became the first English team to win the European Champions Cup. In all, United have won nine league titles, eight FA Cups, the Football League Cup, the European Champions Cup and European Cup-Winners' Cup (1991).
Capacity: 55,000,
Pitch measurements: 116 yd x 76 yd (106m x 69m)

ANFIELD, Liverpool

3

Description: Anfield has been the home of Liverpool since their formation in 1892. The stadium is synonymous with the Kop end, which ceased to be a standing area in 1994. It was the part of the ground where the most fanatical fans stood.
Host club: Liverpool are England's most successful club, and one of the best in Europe. They have won a record 18 League titles, five FA Cups, five Football League Cups, four European Champions Cups, one European Super Cup and two UEFA Cups. In 1986, they completed the double of the League championship and the FA Cup.
Capacity: 41,000
Pitch measurements: 110 yd x 78 yd (101m x 71m)

ELLAND ROAD, Leeds

4

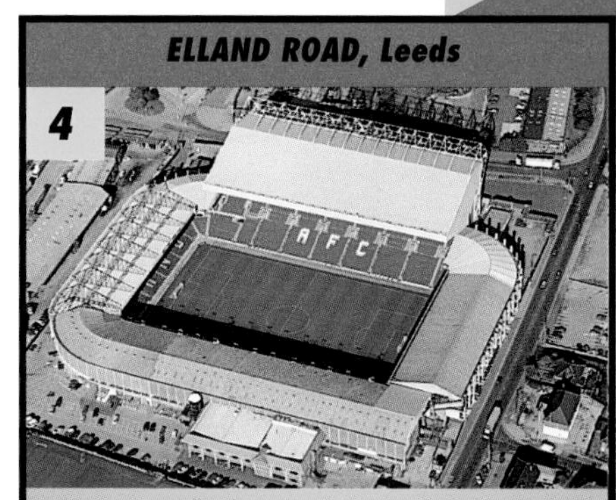

Description: Elland Road is the home of Leeds United, who have played there since their formation. A new pitch was laid in the summer of 1994 with Euro96™ in mind.
Host club: Leeds United rose from the ashes of Leeds City, who were disbanded by Football Association decree in 1919. Leeds have won three League Championships, most recently in 1991–92, two Fairs Cups, the FA Cup and Football League Cup. For all their success in the 1960s and 1970s, Leeds are best known for narrowly missing out on the major prizes, including the 1975 European Champions Cup, when they lost in the Final.
Capacity: 39,000
Pitch measurements: 117 yd x 72 yd (107m x 66m)

VILLA PARK, Birmingham

6

Description: Villa Park, situated in the Aston suburb of Birmingham, became Aston Villa's home in 1897. The ground has undergone a £20 million redevelopment but the old Trinity Road facade remains a monument to the history of both club and stadium.
Host club: Before 1960, Aston Villa recorded six League titles and seven FA Cup victories including the double in 1896–97. Since 1960 the Football League Cup has been won four times, and between 1981 and 1983, the League title, European Champions Cup and European Super Cup were won.
Capacity: 39,000
Pitch measurements: 115 yd x 75 yd (105m x 69m)

CITY GROUND, Nottingham

7

Description: The City Ground (which is actually just outside the city boundaries in West Bridgford) is situated on the banks of the River Trent and has been Nottingham Forest's home since 1898. Nearby are the Trent Bridge cricket ground and the Meadow Lane home of Notts County.
Host club: Nottingham Forest have been League champions once, FA Cup-winners twice and winners of the Football League Cup four times. They also won the European Champions Cup in 1979 and 1980 and the European Super Cup in 1980.
Capacity: 30,500
Pitch measurements: 115 yd x 78 yd (105m x 71m)

WEMBLEY STADIUM, London

8

Description: Wembley is one of the world's most famous football grounds. It has played host to countless famous football occasions, as well as the 1948 Olympic Games. Besides football, rugby league, greyhound racing, American football and speedway have all filled the stadium. Wembley was the UK venue for 1985's Live Aid concert and the stadium is regularly packed for other rock concerts. The stadium was redeveloped in 1960–61, when the roof was added. It has been all-seater since 1990 and has the largest capacity in English football. No club has ever used Wembley as its regular home stadium.
Capacity: 80,000
Pitch measurements: 115 yd x 77 yd (105m x 70m)

THE FINAL COUNTDOWN

The draw for the finals of Euro96™, staged in Birmingham on December 17, 1995, was the moment the tournament really came to life for English fans. Until then, the European Championship had been an event for everyone else on the continent. Now, at last, England were in the spotlight.

UEFA's top men, British TV sports presenters Bob Wilson and Sue Barker, plus 16 children representing the finalist nations turned the Draw into a TV spectacular.

Wilson and Barker introduced the show and reviewed the teams' progress to the finals while the children welcomed viewers and fans from each nation in their own language.

PIECING THE JIGSAW

It was left to UEFA's Swedish president Lennart Johansson, competition vice-president Egidius Braun and general secretary Gerd Aigner to organize the drawing together of the various teams and their groups and venues.

Slowly, the pieces of the jigsaw came together. First the 12 unseeded teams were drawn into the four groups, followed by the four seeds (England, Denmark, Germany and Spain). England's section was designated as Group A — sending them to the Wembley and Birmingham group. The letters B (Leeds and Newcastle), C (Manchester and Liverpool) and D (Sheffield and Nottingham) were then drawn against the other three groups.

Within minutes the national coaches of the various countries were sharing their opinions as they posed together for a "team photograph". Within hours they were heading for home ... and plotting for their return in June.

BEST LAID PLANS

England, as hosts, are favourites to proceed from Group A. But their task promises to be anything but straightforward given the opposition. Scotland return to Wembley for the first time since 1988, and this rivalry never has gone much with

CHILD'S PLAY ***The Draw was enlivened by 16 children who greeted the finalists in their native tongues***

the relative strengths of the bordering nations at the time. Holland bear happy memories of their last competitive meetings with England in the 1994 World Cup qualifiers, a 2–2 draw at Wembley and a 2–0 win in Rotterdam, while England's only victory since 1969 came in 1982.

Nor should Switzerland be underrated. They may have lost 3–1 to England at Wembley in November but Alain Geiger and Co. are sure to step up a gear under competitive conditions, and they recorded a win and a draw against Scotland in the qualifying competition for the 1994 World Cup. Holland showed their current form in the qualifying playoff game a week before the draw was made.

LET BATTLE COMMENCE ***The national coaches know the finals' groups so the real preparation can begin***

WORST CASE SCENARIOS

Aime Jacquet, manager of France, had hoped that he would at least avoid Spain in the draw. Instead, Spain are top seeds in Group B where their meeting with France at Elland Road, Leeds, is a pivotal second fixture for both teams. It is, of course, also a repeat of the Final of the 1984 Championship.

Bulgaria and Romania, eastern Europe's most successful representatives at the last World Cup complete the group. Jacquet had mixed feelings about these two. Bulgaria have developed a nasty habit of upsetting France in competition over the years. At least France will face Romania buoyed by memories of their 3–1 win in Bucharest last October in the qualifying tournament for Euro96™.

KNOCK-OUT BLOWS

Group C is the heavyweight corner ideally designed to thrill the committed fans used to turning out to watch Manchester United and Liverpool at Old Trafford and Anfield. Germany will start against the Czech Republic without top striker Jürgen Klinsmann, who is suspended from the first game after collecting two yellow cards in the closing stages of the qualifiers.

Italy and Russia turn up the pages of history when they face each other in their opening fixture at Anfield: the two nations (Russia under the guise of the Soviet Union) were group rivals in England at the 1966 World Cup. The Soviets then reached the semi-finals while Italy failed to progress beyond the first round. It took a while for Italy to recover from their 1994 World Cup exertions, but their current form makes them a fearsome proposition.

STORIES TO TELL

The first section to be reported a virtual sell-out was Group D at Sheffield's Hillsborough and Nottingham's City Ground. Denmark open their defence of the title against Portugal in what could be one of the most entertaining of first-round games. Two days later, in Nottingham, it will be fascinating to see whether newcomers Croatia can, against Turkey, justify the high ratings generated by the manner of their qualifying success.

Each of the four nations will bring their own individual story to the group. Denmark, the defending champions, who were ignored four years ago; Croatia, whose players are spread all around Europe, but swear unwavering loyalty to their country; Portugal, the young lions who fear no one and on their day can beat all-comers; and Turkey, newcomers to the finals stage, but who just might upset some lofty reputations.

How They Line Up

GROUP A	GROUP C
ENGLAND	GERMANY
SWITZERLAND	CZECH REPUBLIC
HOLLAND	ITALY
SCOTLAND	RUSSIA

GROUP B	GROUP D
SPAIN	DENMARK
BULGARIA	PORTUGAL
ROMANIA	TURKEY
FRANCE	CROATIA

THE DRAW

THE TWIN TOWERS BECKON

THE SCHEDULE

Chart the progress of Euro96™ on these two pages, so that when the final whistle blows you will have a personal record of the essential statistics of the tournament.

In the first round there are four groups, from which the first two in each group will proceed to the quarter-finals. Space has been allowed for you to fill in the results of the matches and the final placings in each group. All times are British Summer Time.

After the group matches have been completed, the competition will proceed on a straight knock-out system. The teams will not be known until the results of the first round have been determined, but we indicate which Group winners and runners-up will play when and where — all the way through to the final at Wembley on 30 June. Space has been provided for you to fill in all the results, the placings after the first round and full details of the final itself.

The "sudden death" or "golden goal" rule will be introduced in the knock-out stages (from the quarter finals). If the score of a match is level at 90 minutes, extra time will start — and the match will finish as soon as a goal is scored. If no goals have been scored after two periods of 15 minutes' extra time, then a penalty shoot-out will follow.

Group A

Date	Time	Venue	Fixture	Score
June 8	3.00	Wembley	England vs. Switzerland	1 – 1
June 10	4.30	Birmingham	Holland vs. Scotland	0 – 0
June 13	7.30	Birmingham	Switzerland vs. Holland	0 – 2
June 15	3.00	Wembley	Scotland vs. England	0 – 2
June 18	7.30	Birmingham	Scotland vs. Switzerland	1 – 0
June 18	7.30	Wembley	Holland vs. England	1 – 4

Final Table

	Team	P	W	D	L	F	A	Pts
1	England	3	2	1	0	7	2	7
2	Holland	3	1	1	1	3	4	4
3	Scotland	3	1	1	1	1	2	4
4	Switzerland	3	0	1	2	1	4	1

Group B

Date	Time	Venue	Fixture	Score
June 9	2.30	Leeds	Spain vs. Bulgaria	1 – 1
June 10	7.30	Newcastle	Romania vs. France	0 – 1
June 13	4.30	Newcastle	Bulgaria vs. Romania	1 – 0
June 15	6.00	Leeds	France vs. Spain	1 – 1
June 18	4.30	Newcastle	France vs. Bulgaria	3 – 1
June 18	4.30	Leeds	Romania vs. Spain	1 – 2

Final Table

	Team	P	W	D	L	F	A	Pts
1	France	3	2	1	0	5	2	7
2	Spain	3	1	2	0	4	3	5
3	Bulgaria	3	1	1	1	3	4	4
4	Romania	3	0	0	3	1	4	0

Group C

Date	Time	Venue	Fixture	Score
June 9	5.00	Manchester	Germany vs. Czech Republic	2 – 0
June 11	4.30	Liverpool	Italy vs. Russia	2 – 1
June 14	7.30	Liverpool	Czech Republic vs. Italy	2 – 1
June 16	3.00	Manchester	Russia vs. Germany	0 – 3
June 19	7.30	Liverpool	Russia vs. Czech Republic	3 – 3
June 19	7.30	Manchester	Italy vs. Germany	0 – 0

Final Table

	Team	P	W	D	L	F	A	Pts
1	Germany	3	2	1	0	5	0	7
2	Czech Republic	3	1	1	1	5	6	4
3	Italy	3	1	1	1	3	3	4
4	Russia	3	0	1	2	4	8	1

Group D

Date	Time	Venue	Fixture	Score
June 9	7.30	Sheffield	Denmark vs. Portugal	1 – 1
June 11	7.30	Nottingham	Turkey vs. Croatia	0 – 1
June 14	4.30	Nottingham	Portugal vs. Turkey	1 – 0
June 16	6.00	Sheffield	Croatia vs. Denmark	3 – 0
June 19	4.30	Nottingham	Croatia vs. Portugal	0 – 3
June 19	4.30	Sheffield	Turkey vs. Denmark	0 – 3

Final Table

	Team	P	W	D	L	F	A	Pts
1	Portugal	3	2	1	0	5	1	7
2	Croatia	3	2	0	1	4	3	6
3	Denmark	3	1	1	1	4	4	4
4	Turkey	3	0	0	3	0	5	0

THE SCHEDULE

Quarter – Finals

Date June 22 | **Time** 3.00 | **Venue** Wembley

Fixture
Runners-up Group B vs. Winners Group A

Score
Spain (2) 0 – 0 (4) England

Date June 22 | **Time** 6.30 | **Venue** Liverpool

Fixture
Winners Group B vs. Runners-up Group A

Score
France (5) 0 – 0 (4) Holland

Date June 23 | **Time** 3.00 | **Venue** Manchester

Fixture
Winners Group C vs. Runners-up Group D

Score
Germany 2 – 1 Croatia

Date June 23 | **Time** 6.30 | **Venue** Birmingham

Fixture
Runners-up Group C vs. Winners Group D

Score
Czech Republic 1 – 0 Portugal

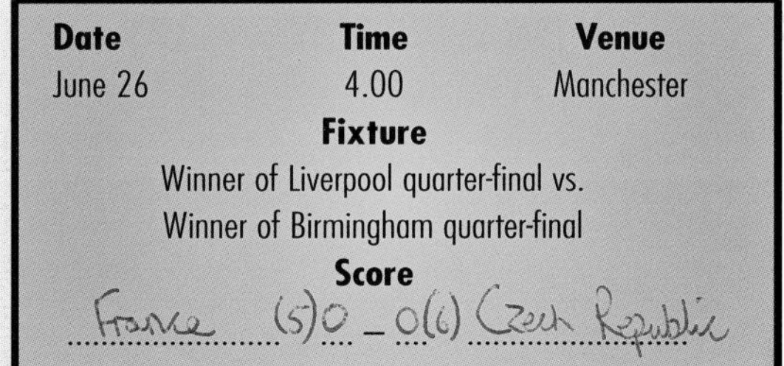

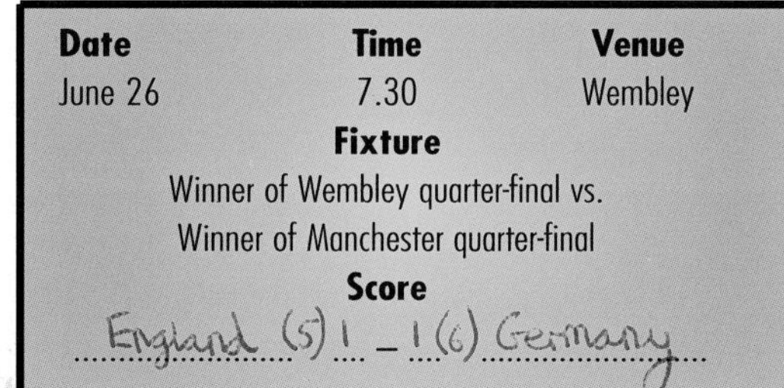

Semi – Finals

Date June 26 | **Time** 4.00 | **Venue** Manchester

Fixture
Winner of Liverpool quarter-final vs.
Winner of Birmingham quarter-final

Score
France (5) 0 – 0 (6) Czech Republic

Date June 26 | **Time** 7.30 | **Venue** Wembley

Fixture
Winner of Wembley quarter-final vs.
Winner of Manchester quarter-final

Score
England (5) 1 – 1 (6) Germany

VENUE OF LEGENDS ***Wembley, host of the Euro96™ Final, has already staged World Cup and Olympic finals***

FINAL

Date June 30 | **Time** 7.00 | **Venue** Wembley

Score
Czech Republic 1 – 1 Germany

Extra time 0–1

Scorers
Berger (pen) | Bierhoff (2)

Euro Superstars

The greatest players in Europe will be on show at Euro96™ – eager to display their talents to the world and give their country that vital edge which could see their team triumph over the rest of the field on June 30.

In June, on eight grounds around England, 320 young men will hope to add their name to the glittering array of superstars who have lit the European Championship stage in the past 36 years, because these tournaments have been dominated by a selection of legendary footballers.

The first finals, in 1960, saw a triumphant Lev Yashin inspiring the Soviet Union but, four years later, they could not cope with the midfield genius of Spain's Luis Suarez. In 1968, hosts Italy looked to the likes of goalkeeper Dino Zoff and striker Luigi Riva while West Germany, in 1972, owed their success to the burgeoning brilliance of sweeper Franz Beckenbauer, the goal-a-game exploits of Gerd Müller and the midfield magnificence of Gunter Netzer.

Ivo Viktor was Czechoslovakia's goalkeeping hero and Antonin Panenka the midfield maestro in their 1976 win, followed, four years later, by deadly Karl-Heinz Rummenigge of West Germany. In 1984, it was Michel Platini, already long recognized as a genius, who stamped his world-class skills on his home soil as France were champions. Marco Van Basten and Ruud Gullit were just two of the greats who fired Holland in 1988 and 1992 was the international making of Danes Peter Schmeichel and Brian Laudrup.

Who's next

The 1994 World Cup provided some clues, with the accession to superstar status of players such as Bulgaria's Hristo Stoichkov, Romania's Gheorghe Hagi, Italian defender Paolo Maldini, his compatriot Roberto Baggio and Dutchman Dennis Bergkamp. But eight of the Euro96™ teams missed the party in America. So the likes of England's Alan Shearer, Frenchman Marcel Desailly, Paulo Sousa of Portugal and Croatia's Zvonimir Boban will want to capitalize on their opportunity.

That is not to forget, of course, long-established heroes such as Germany's Jürgen Klinsmann, as well as men plotting long overdue returns to the international spotlight, players such as Czech Republic striker Tomas Skuhravy and England's Paul Gascoigne.

Of course, it could just as easily be somebody who comes out of relative obscurity and grabs the moment to become a household hero.

Dennis the menace

DENNIS BERGKAMP

Dennis Bergkamp knows all about top-level challenges in football. He has faced them in Holland, in Italy and in England and Euro96™ may be the stage on which he makes that experience tell.

His gifts have never been in doubt in Holland, though they were dimmed after two years in Italy with Internazionale. His first season in England, with Arsenal, thus entailed rebuilding both form and confidence.

Bergkamp is Holland's heir to the throne of Marco Van Basten. He succeeded Van Basten at Ajax Amsterdam and even followed his path to the Stadio Meazza in Italy – though he played for Inter, rather than rivals Milan.

MISERY IN MILAN

In Italy, Bergkamp never recovered from a spell in his first season when he went three months without a goal and looked a shadow of the player he had been before his £6 million move from Amsterdam. He made few friends and lived a reclusive existence with his wife in a villa outside Milan. The Italian media, never slow to dispense with understanding and sympathy, criticized him mercilessly on both personal and technical levels.

Football has always been a central thread in Bergkamp's life – ever since he was born, in fact, and named after his father's great football hero, Denis Law ("He just didn't realize the name was spelled with one 'n'," says Bergkamp). Bergkamp soon found himself enrolled in the schoolboy section of Ajax, a club with one of the most successful youth set-ups in the world.

TWO TESTS IN ONE WEEK

Coach Johan Cruyff gave him his debut, at the age of 17, in the 1986–87 campaign, in a team featuring Van Basten, and Bergkamp's potential was rated so highly that Ajax even flew him to Sweden for a European tie on the day of the game because he had an important school examination the previous afternoon.

Ajax went on to lift the European Cup-winners' Cup and Bergkamp gained his first taste of European glory after making a brief appearance as a substitute in the Final victory over Lokomotiv Leipzig.

Initially a winger, Bergkamp was switched into a more central role to such effect that he averaged 25 goals a season in his last three terms with Ajax. That is the Bergkamp Dutch fans expect to see once more at Euro96™.

"During all my time at Ajax, Dennis was probably the best striker I ever worked with."
Louis Van Gaal, Ajax Amsterdam coach

MAN ON A MISSION *Dennis Bergkamp wants to use Euro96™ as the stage to prove his critics wrong*

Dennis Bergkamp – Holland

POSITION:	Forward
BORN:	Amsterdam, May 10, 1969
CLUBS:	Ajax Amsterdam, Internazionale (Italy), Arsenal (England)
DEBUT:	vs. Italy, 1990

ZVONIMIR BOBAN

Back in the limelight

Zvonimir Boban could hardly have dreamed, as he watched the 1992 European Championship finals unfold in Sweden, that he would lead a new nation into that very event four years later, and that the World Cup finalists would have been beaten on the way.

In the spring of 1992, Boban was considered a key figure in a Yugoslavia side which was among the favourites to win the European crown. But Yugoslavia were barred from the finals in Sweden and the state imploded into battle-scarred fragments. One such fragment is the new nation of Croatia, which Boban will now lead at Euro96™.

And Croatia will not merely be making up the numbers. They are many observers' favourites, driven not merely by football ambition but by patriotic fervour – and inspired from midfield by their Milan-based mastermind.

Experienced newcomer

Boban will be appearing in his first major senior tournament but he knows about the pressure of international competition, thanks both to his years in Italy and also his rise to stardom in the former Yugoslavia.

DANGER MAN ***Zvonimir Boban has been a world star for almost a decade***

Boban was one of the outstanding members of the Yugoslav team which won the FIFA World Youth Cup in Chile 1987 – along with the likes of Robert Prosinecki, now a team-mate in the Croatian national team. Talent-spotters were soon queuing up at the door and Boban was still only 22 when he quit Dinamo Zagreb for Italy in 1991 after having scored 45 goals in 109 games.

He spent one year at Bari before joining Milan but, once there, he struggled to make his mark. The initial problem was the "three foreigners" restriction in league and Europe at a time when Milan had six imports including Dutchmen Frank Rijkaard, Marco Van Basten and Ruud Gullit.

Wise non-move

Coach Arrigo Sacchi suggested that Boban had the talent to step into the boots of either Gullit or Rijkaard and, despite his infrequent appearances early on, Boban quickly became a crowd favourite thanks to his dangerous shooting at free kicks. But he made no secret of his impatience for a regular first-team slot. At one stage Milan suggested a loan transfer to Marseille, but Boban turned it down. He had enough self-confidence to believe he would soon prove his point.

It was Sacchi's successor, Fabio Capello, who gave Boban a regular first-team opportunity and he was outstanding in the 4–0 victory over Barcelona in the 1994 Champions Cup Final in Barcelona. Boban may be a Croat, and club-mate Dejan Savicevic a Serb, but they blend together perfectly out on the football pitch.

Zvonimir Boban – Croatia

Position:	Midfield
Born:	Imostski, October 8, 1968
Clubs:	Dinamo Zagreb (Yugoslavia), Bari (Italy), Milan (Italy)
Debuts:	Yug, vs. Rep. Ireland, 1988; Croatia, vs. Romania, 1990

"We have a very special national pride. To me, it's like having an extra player on our side"

Zvonimir Boban.

ALESSANDRO DEL PIERO

Young gun

Alessandro Del Piero is the most exciting talent to emerge from within Italy since Roberto Baggio. His talent and potential was such that Juventus decided they could afford to let Baggio go to title rivals Milan. What greater recommendation could Del Piero ask?

Del Piero made his name with Padova in Serie B. One goal in 14 games as an 18-year-old was enough to earn a transfer to Juve in the summer of 1993, and he exploded on Serie A in 1993–94 with five goals in 11 games, including a hat-trick against Parma.

Juve coach Marcello Lippi was reluctant, initially, to rely too heavily on Del Piero but a brilliant volleyed goal against Fiorentina left Italy – and Europe – demanding to see more of the shock-haired 20-year-old.

BLINKERED PASSION

Del Piero makes no secret of his passion for the game. He says: "Nothing else interested me. I can echo what Gianni Rivera once said, 'I'm a happy man because my hobby and my profession are one and the same.'"

Juventus' French star Michel Platini was his boyhood hero and, at 13, his youthful talent among the junior leagues of San Vediamo had earned a substantial following of admirers and scouts. Padova got there first, promising him an education both on and off the pitch.

He found it hard, moving away from home and into a club house with other youngsters. He made friends, but missed his old team-mates and school friends. Only that single-minded dedication to making the football grade brought him through to the notice of Juventus.

GOLDEN BOY ***Alessandro Del Piero models himself on Michel Platini***

ON-OFF TRANSFER

Yet Del Piero might have been starring now for Parma. In the summer of 1994, Juve's new executive director Roberto Bettega faced the challenge of tightening up the club's football finances. Bettega was determined to make a transfer market profit and part of that meant agreeing to Parma's interest in buying midfielder Dino Baggio.

The player was reluctant to go and Juventus decided they would, if necessary, sacrifice a half-share in Del Piero instead. Dino Baggio had second thoughts during the summer of 1994, and his agreement to join Parma meant that Juventus could hold on to Del Piero 100 per cent.

National coach Arrigo Sacchi has no doubt about this new golden boy. So there was Del Piero, in the closing stages of the Euro96™ qualifying campaign, taking over from Roberto Baggio for his country just as he had for his club.

Alessandro 'Alex' Del Piero – Italy

POSITION:	***Forward***
BORN:	***Conegliaro, November 9, 1974***
CLUBS:	***Padova, Juventus***
DEBUT:	***vs. Estonia, 1995***

"Even as a child I was obsessed by the prospect of playing football. Only football."

Alessandro Del Piero.

Ghanaian powerhouse

Only five footballers have won the European Champions Cup with two separate clubs. Only one, however, has won the Cup with two separate clubs in succeeding seasons.

The five double-winners are Ronald Koeman (PSV, Holland, and Barcelona), Frank Rijkaard (Milan and Ajax), Miodrag Belodedici (Steaua Bucharest, Romania, then Red Star Belgrade), Dejan Savicevic (Red Star, then Milan) and Marcel Desailly (Marseille, France, then Milan).

Desailly, the Ghana-born midfielder or defender, is the man who has won the Cup with two different clubs in successive seasons – with Marseille against Milan in 1993 and then for Milan against Barcelona.

A powerhouse either in midfield or defence, Desailly's story is an example of the rags to riches legend which inspires so many youngsters around the world. He never knew his father and was adopted, as a baby, by the original Marcel Desailly, who was French Consul-General. When the young Marcel was only four, the family all came to France, to Nantes.

Desailly was outstanding at football, track and field and tennis. He admired Ed Moses and Yannick Noah but, when it came to making a choice, he followed elder brother Seth and became a football apprentice with Nantes.

Showing versatility

At 18, he turned professional and made his league debut, at right-back against Sochaux. His versatility was already appreciated and, in a UEFA Cup-tie against Torino, he played sweeper in the first leg and stopper in the second.

Few French clubs can match Nantes when it comes to developing outstanding young players. But the time comes when they want to move on and opportunity knocked for Desailly in 1992.

He recalls: "I knew it wouldn't be easy – and it wasn't! It wasn't like Nantes. At Marseille, no one was certain of keeping his place in the team and I wanted to win the league and play in the Champions Cup."

European glory

He did both, and more. Desailly starred in the Marseille side which defeated Milan in the 1993 Final in Munich, shutting the great Marco Van Basten out of the game.

But two weeks after the European triumph, the club was plunged into a match-fixing scandal and subsequent financial disaster. President Bernard Tapie had to sell star players to pay the club's debts. Milan, remembering Desailly's starring role against Van Basten, snapped him up in November 1993.

The French national team have emerged the winners quite as much as Milan.

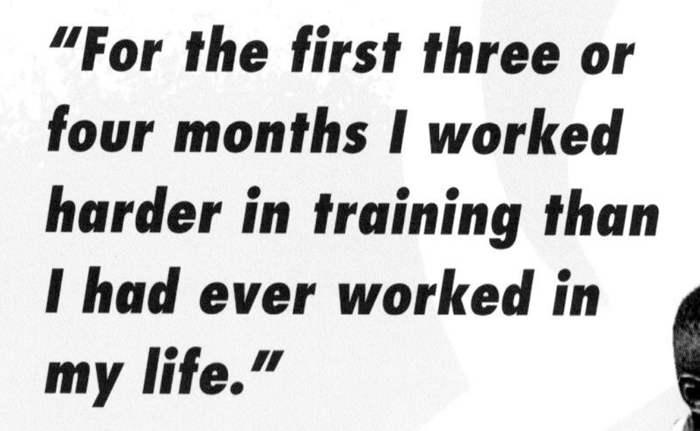

"For the first three or four months I worked harder in training than I had ever worked in my life."

Marcel Desailly, on his early career in Marseille.

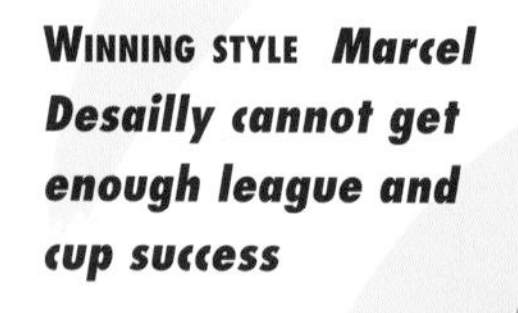

WINNING STYLE ***Marcel Desailly cannot get enough league and cup success***

Marcel Desailly – France

POSITION:	***Midfielder/central defender***
BORN:	***Accra, Ghana, September 7, 1968***
CLUBS:	***Nantes, Marseille, Milan (Italy)***
DEBUT:	***vs. Sweden, 1993***

Joker in the pack

PAUL GASCOIGNE

Paul Gascoigne's England team-mates and coaches love having him on board not only because his practical jokes and simple humour keep them amused and take the edge off competitive pressure, but also Gascoigne, despite all the injuries, retains a singular talent for football at the highest levels.

It was a surprise, in the summer of 1995, when Rangers jumped to the head of the queue to pay the £4.5 million Lazio of Italy wanted for Gascoigne's transfer. His decision to play in Scotland raised some eyebrows in England but, at 28, he was impatient to win trophies and that hunger for success, despite all the distractions of a controversial career, was good news for England.

Born in Gateshead, Gascoigne joined Newcastle United as an apprentice in 1983 and scored 22 goals in 106 league and cup appearances, before Tottenham won the race for his signature in the summer of 1988. Gascoigne's bubbly personality quickly made itself felt at international level. He made his England debut that year, against Denmark and, two years later, he earned worldwide attention at the World Cup finals.

Tears in Turin

Gascoigne's enjoyment of his football, love of the big occasion and pride in playing for England were all encapsulated in the pictures which showed him in tears before the penalty shoot-out following the semi-final against West Germany in Turin. Gascoigne's upset was in being shown a yellow card which would have ruled him out of the Final if England got there.

Of course, they did not – but Gascoigne had captured the admiration and sympathy of the world in general and Italian football in particular.

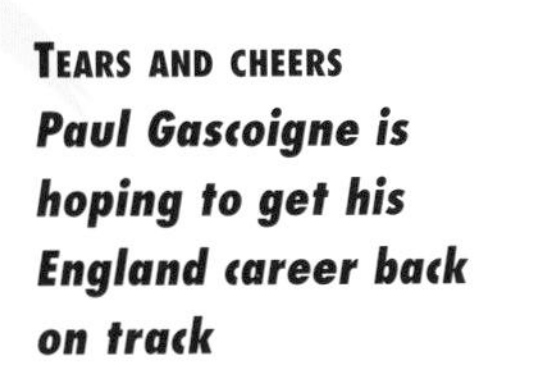

TEARS AND CHEERS
Paul Gascoigne is hoping to get his England career back on track

Injury setbacks

Lazio pounced. Spurs, in financial difficulty, agreed to a £5.5 million sale. But, before the deal could be completed, Gascoigne wrecked a knee in a reckless tackle in the 1991 FA Cup Final. The injury, compounded by further damage away from the football pitch, cost him a year out of the game.

The eventual move to Italy made too many headlines of the wrong sort. Gascoigne struggled with his fitness and he and Lazio came to a parting of the ways after he had missed a second year with a serious injury, this time a broken leg suffered in training.

Gascoigne will need to steer clear of both injury and controversy if England are to return to the international forefront.

"Gazza is a great talent, a great character. He still has so much to offer English football."

Dino Zoff, Lazio coach-turned-president.

Paul Gascoigne – England

Position:	*Midfield*
Born:	*Gateshead, May 27, 1967*
Clubs:	*Newcastle, Tottenham Hotspur, Lazio (Italy), Rangers (Scotland)*
Debut:	*vs. Denmark, 1988*

JULEN GUERRERO

Basque Warrior

The directors of Athletic Bilbao never doubted the qualities of the young Julen Guerrero. By the age of 21 he held a contract which provided him with a basic salary of £250,000 per year and which placed a transfer buy-out value on his head of £6 million.

Guerrero's name means "Warrior", and Athletic Bilbao's fans have been delighted to watch his progress in the service of one of Spain's oldest and most respected clubs.

Guerrero exploded on the Spanish league in 1992. In January, 1993, Guerrero was called up by national coach Javier Clemente – another former Bilbao favourite – for a friendly match against Mexico. Guerrero became, at 19 years 20 days, the second-youngest international debutant in Spanish football history.

SHOWERED WITH AWARDS

At the end of that season Guerrero was voted Young Player of the Year by the weekly magazine *Don Balon* and celebrated by scoring twice in Spain's 2–0 win over Lithuania in June 1993. Two more goals followed three months later in a 2–0 win over Chile. Guerrero thus had no problem earning a place in Spain's World Cup squad for USA '94.

Fans nicknamed him the "Spanish Laudrup", after Real Madrid's experienced Dane. But Guerrero himself shrugged off comparisons.

"It's true I have always been a great admirer of Michael Laudrup," he said. "What we do have in common, I believe, is that we both go out for every match confident and determined to reach the final whistle on the winning side."

FLOATING LIKE A BUTTERFLY

Guerrero is neither an out-and-out striker nor is he an easily-definable midfield general. He prefers to hover somewhere between the two, upsetting both opposing defenders and midfielders. Defenders do not know whether to go forward and leave gaps at the back while midfield opponents do not want to sacrifice their own potential influence within the game by spending the 90 minutes tied to Guerrero's bootlaces.

Guerrero's "floating" role at Bilbao, where he has long been free to follow his own attacking instincts, was one of the reasons he was not always an automatic choice for national team coach Clemente, who prefers a well-structured tactical approach.

Guerrero says: "I love playing for the national side. The team spirit and morale among the players are phenomenal. I honestly believe that, under Clemente, we can go on from where we left off at USA '94 to achieve even greater things."

Julen Guerrero – Spain

POSITION:	*Midfield*
BORN:	*Portugalete, January 7, 1974*
CLUB:	*Athletic Bilbao*
DEBUT:	*vs. Mexico, 1993*

"I would rather people remembered me for my own strengths and abilities."

Julen Guerrero, on comparisons with Michael Laudrup.

SPANISH PRIDE ***Julen Guerrero provides the missing link in attack***

Maradona of the Carpathians

Gheorghe Hagi, Barcelona's Romanian midfielder, is already thinking ahead to his retirement.

The so-called "Maradona of the Carpathians" has invested some of his earnings from his years in Spain and Italy in a dental practice back in Bucharest. Not that Hagi is qualified to fill holes in patients' teeth, but he has built a comfortable fortune from finding holes in opposing football teams' defences.

Hagi began with his local club, FC Constanta, and swiftly moved up the domestic ladder. He was brought to the Romanian capital with Sportul Studentesc and was subsequently stolen away, on political orders, by the army club, Steaua Bucharest. A youth international at 15, he made his senior debut in a 0–0 draw against Norway in Oslo at 18.

In esteemed company

Hagi's left foot was compared with that of Hungarian great Ferenc Puskas. It brought him 100 league goals while still a teenager, he was twice the league's leading marksman and scored 76 goals in 97 league games before he joined Real Madrid for a Romanian record £2 million after the 1990 World Cup.

In his first season, he disappointed fans and management alike, scoring only three goals, and while the second season brought 14 goals, it was not enough to enable Madrid to break Barcelona's stranglehold on the Spanish league title.

In 1992, Madrid, impatient and frustrated, sold Hagi to Italian club Brescia, who had been establishing a Romanian football colony with coach Mircea Lucescu and Hagi's fellow internationals Dorin Mateut, Ioan Sabau and Florin Raducioiu. Hagi says: "Brescia had just been promoted and I loved the place. All my friends were there."

An American tale

But Hagi had greater ambitions than Brescia could fulfil. He had not lived up to his reputation when Romania reached the second round of the 1990 World Cup, and he had his sights set on USA '94, and a global stage on which to display his undoubted talent.

In Romania's opening match against Colombia, Hagi scored an astonishing goal with a long angled lob from out on the left which swirled beyond the goalkeeper and inside the far post. It was the start of a remarkable series of displays which took Romania to the quarter-finals and earned Hagi a place in just about everyone's "team of the tournament."

Hagi's brilliant play earned him another lucrative transfer, with Barcelona bringing him back to Spain – the ideal foundation from which to prepare for the high-profile challenge offered by Euro96™.

"I could happily have finished my career with Brescia." *Gheorghe Hagi, on his time in Italy.*

Gheorghe Hagi – Romania	
Position:	Midfield
Born:	Constanta, February 5, 1965
Clubs:	FC Constanta, Sportul Studentesc, Steaua Bucharest, Real Madrid (Spain), Brescia (Italy), Barcelona (Spain)
Debut:	vs. Norway, 1983

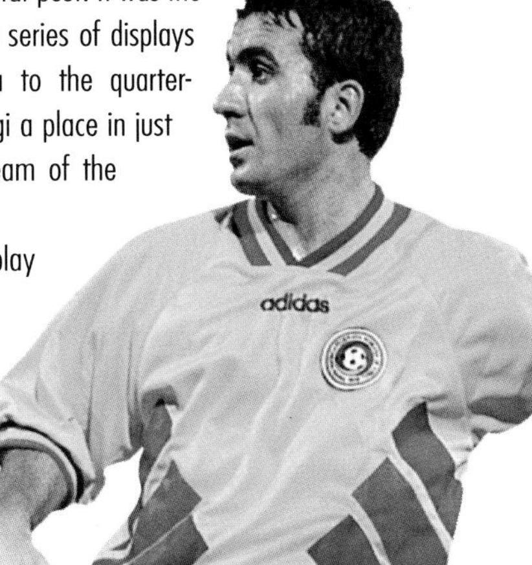

Midfield bite
Gheorghe Hagi cannot wait to get his teeth into Euro96™

HAKAN SUKUR

Man of action

Nedo Sonetti, Torino's coach when the club signed Turkish marksman Hakan Sukur in 1995, had no doubts. He said: "Hakan, without any doubt, has all the quality to become a great player."

However, proving the point has not proved a simple matter for Turkey's gangling centre-forward. Hakan top-scored for Turkey with five goals in their qualifying campaign and led his country's attack with a dynamic spirit which mirrored the all-action style of his favourite film star, Jean-Claude Van Damme.

But he found his transfer to Italy too much. Within five months Galatasaray had bought him back for the same £3 million they received from Torino in the summer.

Simply, Hakan never overcame his homesickness. He says: "It was hard being so far away from Galatasaray, my old club, and all my friends there. I was a fan of the club from childhood. It's hard when you go to a new country and don't understand the language. I spent hours each evening phoning home."

HOME IS WHERE THE HEART LIES

Hardly surprisingly then, Hakan was sold back to Galatasaray after only five months in Italy. Now, at Euro96™, he has the opportunity to demonstrate exactly what Torino and Italian football have been missing.

Hakan was raised in the town of Sakarya, an hour's flight from Istanbul. His father had played for the local team in Sakarya in the second and third divisions and later became general manager, so it was inevitable that Hakan, aged just seven, joined the club's junior section.

Although he was a promising basketball player, football was his passion and he became a fan, from afar, of Galatasaray. As Hakan grew older so he and his friends would hitchhike to Istanbul to see Galatasaray play.

TEENAGE SUPERSTAR

At 16, Hakan made his debut for Sakaryaspor. At 18, the "Young Bull of the Bosphorus" moved to Bursaspor. Two years later, a dream came true for Hakan when Galatasaray bought him to replace the legendary Tanju Colak.

Hakan's national team debut followed soon after. At long last Turkey, who had suffered an international goal drought for years, had a centre-forward who promised the goals which would put the country on the international map. Hakan's steady strike rate drew spies from some of Europe's top clubs, among them Belgians Anderlecht, Paris Saint-Germain from France and, of course, Torino.

But Turkey is where Hakan has proved his heart lies.

"Hakan is a real professional. Serious, dedicated, and an outstanding natural athlete."

Nedo Sonetti, former Torino coach.

Hakan Sukur – Turkey	
POSITION:	Striker
BORN:	Sakarya, September 1, 1971
CLUBS:	Sakaryaspor, Bursaspor, Galatasaray, Torino (Italy), Galatasaray
DEBUT:	vs. Luxembourg, 1992

TICKET TO RIDE
Hakan is the answer to the prayers of the Turkish fans

Winger with a sense of purpose

Andrei Kanchelskis is driven down the right wing for Russia and Everton by a force beyond football ambition – an awareness of the tangible value of success for his family back home in the Ukraine city of Donetsk.

ANDREI KANCHELSKIS

SECURITY ALERT *Andrei Kanchelskis proved a bargain buy*

Kanchelskis has always looked beyond the immediate challenge of the next match to the days when his career will be football history.

He regularly sends airline tickets to the his homeland in the Ukraine, to allow his mother-in-law the chance to visit her daughter Inna and grandson Andrei, Junior, in England. Andrei, Senior's, mother earns just £10 a month working in a factory making car radios.

SECURITY CONSCIOUS

That is why he has pursued security through his transfers from Shakhtyor Donetsk to Manchester United and then on to Everton. That is why, after the collapse of the Soviet Union, he took up the offer to continue his international career with the new Russian state rather than with his native Ukraine. That was why Kanchelskis was one of the players who rebelled against the management of Pavel Sadyrin during the 1994 World Cup qualifying campaign.

Kanchelskis sets high standards on and off the pitch and Italy's Juventus, Spain's Sevilla and Germany's Bayer Leverkusen were among the interested spectators during the transfer tussle which ended last summer with Kanchelskis quitting Old Trafford for Goodison Park.

Andrei Kanchelskis – Russia

POSITION:	Winger
BORN:	Donetsk, Ukraine, January 23, 1969
CLUBS:	Zvezda Kirovograd, Kiev Dynamo, Shakhtyor Donetsk, Manchester United (England), Everton (England)
DEBUTS:	USSR, vs. Poland, 1989, Russia, vs. Luxembourg, 1993

Kanchelskis began his career with Soviet second division side Zvezda Kirovograd, had a short spell with Kiev Dynamo and moved to Shakhtyor in 1990. Kanchelskis made his Soviet debut as a substitute in a 1–1 draw against Poland in August, 1989, and was the Soviet Union's three-goal top scorer in the 1992 European qualifiers.

CULT HERO

Manchester United manager Alex Ferguson knew he had a bargain when he signed Kanchelskis for just £500,000 from Donetsk in the spring of 1991. In four years, he became a cult figure with United's fans. Kanchelskis scored 28 goals in 123 Premiership matches and contributed mightily to the historic 1994 league and cup double.

Kanchelskis once said: "The economic situation at home is very bad. I want to go back when I finish playing but to do that I must secure my future financially."

As Kanchelskis is well aware, he could have few better qualifications to take home with him, when he does finally retire, than the status which comes with having been acclaimed a champion of Europe.

"I would like to be a coach and work with young players in the Ukraine." *Andrei Kanchelskis.*

JÜRGEN KLINSMANN

Leading from the front

It is a measure of the talent exhibited by Jürgen Klinsmann that his single season in English football ended with the award of the Footballer of the Year from the Football Writers' Association.

The award ranked Klinsmann up alongside previous winners such as Stanley Matthews, Tom Finney, Bobby Charlton and Bobby Moore as an immortal of the English game. The weight of Klinsmann's achievement was made clearer from the fact that only two other foreign players had previously won the Footballer of the Year award – compatriot Bert Trautmann, in 1956, and Dutchman Frans Thyssen in 1981.

Such awards acknowledge that Klinsmann is not only a great marksman but also an inspirational footballer. Those qualities were recognized by German national coach Berti Vogts during the qualifying campaign to reach Euro96™, when he turned to Klinsmann to take over the captaincy after injury ruled out Lothar Matthäus. He reacted to the honour in typical style.

Goals galore

Not only did Klinsmann lead Germany to the finals for the seventh successive time, but he was their leading goalscorer, with nine of their 27 goals along the way.

Jürgen Klinsmann – Germany

POSITION:	Striker
BORN:	Boblingen, July 30, 1964
CLUBS:	Kickers Stuttgart, VfB Stuttgart, Internazionale (Italy), Monaco (France), Tottenham Hotspur (England), Bayern Munich
DEBUT:	vs. Brazil, 1987

"Klinsi" exploded on German football in 1986–87. He had begun with Stuttgart Kickers then crossed the city to VfB Stuttgart with whom he earned international recognition for the first time in a 1–1 draw against Brazil in December, 1987.

Klinsmann was Germany's 19-goal top scorer in 1988 – he was voted German Footballer of the Year and was West Germany's biggest success at the same year's European Championship. He led Stuttgart to the UEFA Cup Final in 1989, before moving to Italy with Internazionale in 1990.

Leaving his mark

Two more years and he was helping Germany to World Cup success in Italy. Here, he played perhaps the game of his life in their 2–1 second round win over Holland in Milan.

Klinsmann left Inter for Monaco in 1992, transferring to Tottenham in 1994, before being lured home by the irresistible opportunity of playing for Franz Beckenbauer at Bayern. Within a few days of his return Klinsmann was voted runner-up behind Matthias Sammer in Germany's own Footballer of the Year poll.

Justification arrived quickly with those decisive goals in the Euro96™ qualifiers and a remarkable hat-trick for Bayern against Benfica of Portugal in the UEFA Cup. Few prizes have escaped Klinsmann but the European Championship is one of them – so far.

HAPPY WANDERER ***Klinsmann was 1995 Footballer of the Year – in England***

"Football is changing and, if we want to be as successful as our past, then our football must change and adapt to new techniques, new tactics and new opponents." Jürgen Klinsmann.

Teenage sensation

Patrick Kluivert, not 20 until the day of the Euro96™ Final, ended 1995 in a daze of his own making. In seven months he had leaped from national fame with Ajax to international superstardom with not only his club but with Holland, too.

He scored the winning goal for Ajax against Milan in the European Champions Cup Final in Vienna in May 1995 – after coming on as a substitute – and the two goals with which the Dutch beat the Republic of Ireland at Anfield, Liverpool, in their European Championship qualifying play-off in December 1995.

The teenager who had long been considered by Ajax as one of their great hopes for the future, had proved their point much sooner than anyone could have dreamed.

Kluivert made his initial impact with Ajax playing wide on the left in attack. But his height, power and football intelligence meant it was only a matter of time before the Dutch champions switched him inside to play more responsible roles. Kluivert approaches Euro96™ still coming to terms with his own explosive success.

DREAM TEEN

He says: "Which teenager can say he has won a national championship, the Champions Cup against Milan – scoring the winning goal – the World Club Cup ... and that he has then scored both goals in his country's most vital match in years?"

The easy answer now is: No-one else. But Kluivert has had to grow up quickly. Not merely has he had to cope with events on the pitch, but a serious, widely-publicized car crash placed Kluivert under police investigation and it took all the player's mental strength – and Ajax's guidance – to help him cope with the anguish.

UNDER THE SPOTLIGHT

Kluivert's football future is bright. He will surely relish the football spotlight offered by the prospect of facing England, Scotland and Switzerland in the group matches at Euro96™. Success in this tournament will confirm Kluivert's status as the top target in Italy.

In the meantime Kluivert is confident that he represents a new generation of Dutch footballers who will dominate the European game for years to come. He says: "It will be my first big tournament. It will not be the end of the world if we do not win. But our team is so young and full of talent that I expect the best perhaps not until the next World Cup in 1998 or even when Holland and Belgium together stage the next European Championship in 2000."

Holland's rivals at Euro96™ should not let such modesty deceive them.

MARKSMAN SUPREME
Kluivert's goals defeated the Irish

"I cannot wait to go out there in England and help show the world what we are capable of."

Patrick Kluivert, on his Dutch team.

Patrick Kluivert – Holland

POSITION:	Striker
BORN:	Amsterdam, July 1, 1976
CLUB:	Ajax Amsterdam
DEBUT:	vs. Czech Republic, 1994

PATRICK KLUIVERT

MICHAEL LAUDRUP

Living up to his promise

If anyone ever doubted Michael Laudrup's claims to be considered one of the world's great players, they should study Real Madrid's 1995 revival.

Throughout his career Laudrup, possibly Denmark's finest product, has needed the inspiration of a new challenge every few years to re-ignite the talent which once made him the most-coveted teenager in Europe.

Born in 1964, Laudrup – elder brother of Brian – played first in the boys section of the Vanlose club in Copenhagen at which father Finn had begun. At 14, he joined the youth section at Brondby before moving temporarily to KB Copenhagen, the country's oldest and most respected outfit. Laudrup made his league debut for KB at 17, against Aarhus, then returned to Brondby – again under the tutelage of his father.

FAMOUS FATHER, FAMOUS SONS

Finn Laudrup was a former Danish international who was convinced about his son's potential, and was not surprised when the phone began to ring with a string of calls from scouts and clubs. Laudrup's natural talent was so evident that word spread beyond Denmark. All Europe's top clubs came to watch. It came down to a choice between Juventus and Liverpool.

The Laudrups liked the terms Liverpool offered but they opted for Juventus – who lent Laudrup to Lazio before recalling him in time to win the 1985 World Club Cup. A year later, Laudrup starred on a world stage again. At the 1986 World Cup finals in Mexico he contributed perhaps the finest performance of his career in the Danes' 6–1 thrashing of Uruguay.

Back in Europe, Laudrup grew increasingly discontented with Italian football and moved on to Barcelona with whom he has won both the European Champions and Cup-winners' Cups as well as four Spanish league titles under Johan Cruyff.

Michael Laudrup – Denmark	
Position:	*Midfield / forward*
Born:	*Copenhagen, June 15, 1964*
Clubs:	*KB Copenhagen, Brondby, Juventus (Italy), Barcelona (Spain), Real Madrid (Spain)*
Debut:	*vs. Czechoslovakia, 1982*

PEACE MAKER *Michael Laudrup is back in favour with Denmark*

FALLING OUT

Eventually, Laudrup and Cruyff fell out. The last straw for Laudrup was being omitted from Barcelona's team for the 1994 Champions Cup Final. Without him, the Spaniards were humiliated, 4–0, by Milan. Within weeks he had signed a contract with Barça's most deadly rivals, Real Madrid.

Cruyff is not the only coach whose views Laudrup has not always shared. A disagreement with Denmark boss Richard Moller Nielsen meant Laudrup was absent from the team which won the 1992 European Championship.

The two men made their peace afterwards then, ironically, Denmark failed to qualify for the 1994 World Cup finals. Of course, there's still Euro96™.

"For me, the tangible rewards have never been an end in themselves. Wherever I have played what has mattered most has been enjoying the football itself." *Michael Laudrup.*

It's a family affair

Dynasty is more than a soap opera to Italian football, it's a family show of the most remarkable kind – and the current star is Milan left-back Paolo Maldini.

His father, Cesare, is coach to the Italian team which won the 1994 European Under-21 Championship. Now his son hopes to complete a rare European double and add the European Championship to the European Champions Cups he collected in 1989, 1990 and 1994.

Maldini, senior was himself captain of Milan's first European Cup-winning team at Wembley in 1963 against Benfica. It was the first of five Champions Cups which would fall to the Italian giants in 31 years – and the Maldini family has bridged that football generation gap.

Cesare's son, Paolo, was at left-back against Steaua Bucharest in 1989 and Benfica in 1990 and centre-back against Barcelona in 1994. No prouder spectator sat up in the stands on those May evenings than father Cesare. Yet, as Paolo has readily confessed, there were no favours along the way. If anything, his father worked him harder than the rest of the Milan youth team.

Paolo is taller, leaner and quicker than his father and has already far outstripped him in terms of international appearances.

In famous footsteps

He follows in the great tradition by which Italian football, despite its defensive image, has developed some of the finest attacking fullbacks in the modern game. Giacinto Facchetti, who scored 62 goals for Italy and Internazionale in the 1960s and 1970s, was the model on which many would-be successors based their game.

Maldini has so far scored little more than a dozen goals for his club but he has time on his side – though it's unlikely he will remain a fullback for much longer. Arrigo Sacchi, the coach who launched him at Milan, considers Maldini's long-term future lies in the heart of defence, just like his father.

"My father taught me everything. I wanted to succeed for myself; but I owed it to him." Paolo Maldini.

Paolo Maldini – Italy

Position:	Left-back
Born:	Milan, June 26, 1968
Club:	Milan
Debut:	vs. Yugoslavia, 1988

Starting young

Maldini made his Milan debut, away to Udinese, in January, 1985, at the age of 16 and his full international debut as a substitute for Italy in a goalless draw against Yugoslavia in March, 1988. Three months later, he was starring for Italy at the European Championship finals in West Germany.

It was obvious from early on that Maldini would be a fixture on the international scene for years to come. In 1990, he won a third-place medal at the World Cup in Italy and was then a runner-up four years later in Pasadena.

Leading light ***Paolo Maldini will captain Italy in the Euro96™ finals***

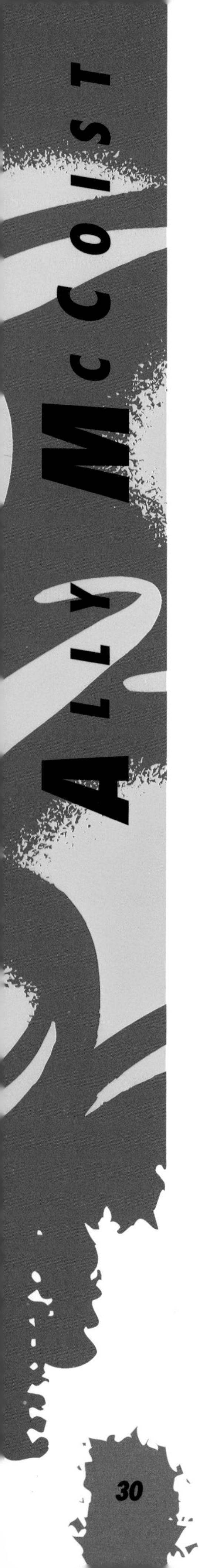

Marksman supreme

Ally McCoist, Scottish marksman supreme, will return to England for Euro96™ as a hero. That would be very different from the circumstances under which a much younger McCoist left England, to return to Rangers, in the summer of 1983.

Then, McCoist's two-year experience of playing in England was not the happiest. He scored only eight goals in 56 league games. He now returns under a new guise, the "Peter Pan of football", so dubbed by manager Craig Brown, after McCoist's crucial goal against Greece at Hampden Park last autumn.

RECORD BREAKER ***Ally McCoist has a nose for important goals for club and country***

QUICK STRIKE

McCoist took just 60 seconds to mark his substitute's return from a 28-month international exile through injury by heading Scotland's winner against the Greeks. It was his 16th goal in his 47th international, and it placed him within three appearances of a place in the official Scottish Football Association's Hall of Fame – an honour reserved for players with 50 caps or more.

Later Brown said: "Ally still loves his football as much as ever and age is no reason why he shouldn't be at the finals."

McCoist has come a long way since the days when, despite playing for Lanarkshire, he never quite made the Scottish schoolboys team. He was, scouts thought, too small. But St Johnstone gambled on his natural talent. They, too, thought him too frail to play up front so he played his first full season in midfield. Next season, manager Alec Rennie experimented with McCoist in attack and, almost overnight, he was recognized as different class.

WOE ON WEARSIDE

His fledgling reputation spread quickly to England. Sunderland won the transfer race in the summer of 1981, paying St Johnstone £320,000 – a massive fee then, especially for a teenager. But the goal avalanche never came. That had to wait until McCoist returned to Scotland with Rangers after two years.

The Rangers' manager was John Greig, who had always had faith in McCoist. He brought the player home to Glasgow and was the man with most reason to celebrate when McCoist scored a hat-trick as Rangers defeated old rivals Celtic in the Scottish League Cup Final of 1983.

Selection for Scotland's under-21, and then the senior national team, followed swiftly. Now he totals more than 300 goals for Rangers and has twice been hailed as Europe's leading league goalscorer.

What chance is there of him becoming the European Championship's leading marksman, too?

> **"Ally may be well past 30, but age is no barrier if the player is good enough and determined enough."**
>
> *Craig Brown, Scotland coach.*

Ally McCoist – Scotland	
POSITION:	Striker
BORN:	Glasgow, September 24, 1962
CLUBS:	St Johnstone, Sunderland (England), Rangers
DEBUT:	vs. Holland, 1986

MATTHIAS SAMMER

Sweeper from the East

Matthias Sammer could not have been on the receiving end of a greater compliment than that paid by veteran international team-mate Lothar Matthäus.

The Bayern Munich skipper, talking about his prospects of recovering from injury in time to appear at Euro96™, said: "Ideally I would like to play sweeper but perhaps that is not possible now Sammer is there."

Such an acknowledgement from a rival such as Matthäus was music to the ears of the former East German international who now plays such a significant role not only with his club, Borussia Dortmund, but with the German national team.

LIKE FATHER, LIKE SON

This situation would have been impossible when Sammer was coming up through the ranks at Dynamo Dresden in the old East Germany.

Matthias's father, Klaus, played for Dresden and East Germany and had barely retired before son Matthias was making his own reputation, in the same position, with the same club and the national team. In 1986, young Sammer guided East Germany to the European youth title. He rose rapidly into the senior national squad, helped Dresden win the championship in 1989 and then the league and cup double a year later.

That summer also brought the collapse of the Berlin Wall – and Sammer was immediately brought west by Stuttgart. He became, the following December, the first East German to play for unified Germany in a 4–0 defeat of Switzerland.

Sammer held his place for a season then displeased coach Berti Vogts by pulling out of a friendly against England, citing injury, but played a league match the next weekend. He was dropped and was not recalled to the squad until the 1992 European Championships.

TROUBLED TIMES

The Championships were an unhappy time for Sammer. He failed to find his form and, in the shock Final defeat by Denmark, was substituted by Vogts at half-time. It was the start of a dismal nine months.

Internazionale had already agreed to buy Sammer from Stuttgart, but he never came to grips with either the lifestyle or the football in Italy and Dortmund brought him home in mid-season. The high fee was ridiculed as being over the top for a midfielder-cum-sweeper, but when Sammer masterminded Dortmund's 1995 league title success, the laughing stopped.

Now a unified Germany expects him to inspire similar success with the national team.

Matthias Sammer – Germany

POSITION:	Midfield/sweeper
BORN:	Dresden, September 5, 1967
CLUBS:	Dynamo Dresden, Stuttgart, Internazionale (Italy), Borussia Dortmund
DEBUTS:	East Germany, vs. France, 1986; Germany, vs. Switzerland, 1990

MR VERSATILITY
Matthias Sammer can play at sweeper or in midfield

"I try to be honest about my football. That makes me my own worst critic!"

Matthias Sammer.

CIRIACO SFORZA

Cosmopolitan all-rounder

"Ciri" Sforza is one of Europe's most wanted men. His all-round talent has attracted the attention of clubs and coaches throughout western Europe. Among the general public, Sforza has been underrated. But not among his fellow professionals.

In Switzerland, he was squabbled over by Grasshopper-Club and Aarau. Then, he was wanted in Germany and signed by Kaiserslautern, before Bayern Munich claimed him in a transfer which had been agreed during the previous season.

Barely had Sforza begun his new career in Bavaria before he was being linked with Italian giants Internazionale – where his former national team coach Roy Hodgson had taken over late in 1995.

COSMOPOLITAN MAN

Sforza represents Switzerland's cosmopolitan mixture. Born to Italian parents who had emigrated to Aarau in the 1960s, he was the third of four children and the only boy.

Sforza is a midfield anchor for Switzerland and Bayern Munich. He possesses a mixture of tough tackling, tactical discipline, high-class technique and powerful shot. His talent has never been in doubt, ever since his first amateur steps with minor Swiss clubs Villmergen and Wohlen in the early and mid-1980s.

In 1986, Sforza, still only 16, was signed by Switzerland's greatest club, Grasshopper of Zurich. He made his league debut that year, becoming the youngest professional player ever to appear in the Swiss championship. Sforza spent three seasons with Grasshopper, then moved to home-town club Aarau, before returning to the Hoppers in 1990.

ANCHOR MAN ***Ciri Sforza has the skills everybody wants***

REGULAR AS CLOCKWORK

The following year he helped Grasshopper win the league and was promoted by then national boss Uli Stielike for his international debut. Sforza went from strength to strength with German and Italian clubs competing for his services – the Italians attracted, among other things, by his family background which means he would not suffer the lifestyle confusion which hinders the progress of so many foreign arrivals.

Hodgson duly succeeded Stielike as national manager of Switzerland. He admired Sforza's ability and saw his potential as a key member of the team, but also felt that the midfielder was sometimes short on commitment and endeavour. Similarly, Sforza felt Hodgson was too demanding and critical.

Misunderstanding soon changed to mutual respect, especially after Sforza's transfer to the full-time professional world of German football with Kaiserslautern. Euro96™ could see Sforza revealed as one of Europe's most coveted midfielders.

"I cannot remember when I was without a football. I started playing in a boys team when I was only seven. It's been like ... my destiny." Ciri Sforza.

Ciriaco Sforza – Switzerland

POSITION:	Midfield
BORN:	Aarau, March 2, 1970
CLUBS:	Grasshopper, Aarau, Grasshopper, Kaiserslautern (Germany), Bayern Munich (Germany)
DEBUT:	vs. Czechoslovakia, 1991

Archetypal centre-forward

The burden of playing under the mantle of "the new Geoff Hurst" is an almost unbearable one for any England striker. From the way he plays, it seems that nobody has told Alan Shearer of it.

Hurst scored the historic hat-trick which brought England victory in the 1966 World Cup Final. Scoring goals has become a lot tougher since those days, but Shearer – generally acknowledged as the finest all-round attack leader in 1990s' English football – has long been the man most likely to make up the shortfall.

Shearer scored on his debuts for Southampton, Blackburn Rovers and for England – in a 2–0 win against France in 1992. But though he made his footballing name in the south of England, Shearer hails from Gosforth, in the footballing hotbed that is North-East England, where he learned his football playing in the streets.

He was marked out for stardom from his earliest days. Naturally, he graduated to a trial with Newcastle United. But, because he also tried out as a goalkeeper, they let him slip through their fingers.

Debut hat-trick

Southampton's own scouting system picked up where Newcastle's left off. At 16, he was an apprentice, more than 300 miles from home, and working and training as hard as he could. His reward was a 4–2 debut win over Arsenal in which he scored a sensational hat-trick. At 17 years 240 days, he remains the youngest hat-trick scorer in the top division.

Shearer's strike rate with Southampton of 23 goals in 118 league games attracted attention from the likes of Liverpool and Manchester United. But it was Blackburn Rovers, courtesy of wealthy chairman Jack Walker, who sealed the deal. A domestic record of £3.3 million was the price for the man on whom Terry Venables has rested his attacking ambitions for Euro96™.

Venables says: "He's so good it's frightening. He can score goals with his head, with his right foot and with his left foot."

Injury strikes

Shearer has had his share of injury problems. But his most serious injury, snapping a cruciate knee ligament, was more accident than foul. The occasion was Boxing Day, 1992, and it was not until the following season that Shearer played again.

Shearer ended the 1993–94 season with his confidence restored, and the next campaign proved the point. His "SAS" partnership with Chris Sutton yielded 49 of Blackburn's 80 goals (Shearer claimed 34) and, on top of all that, the Premiership crown.

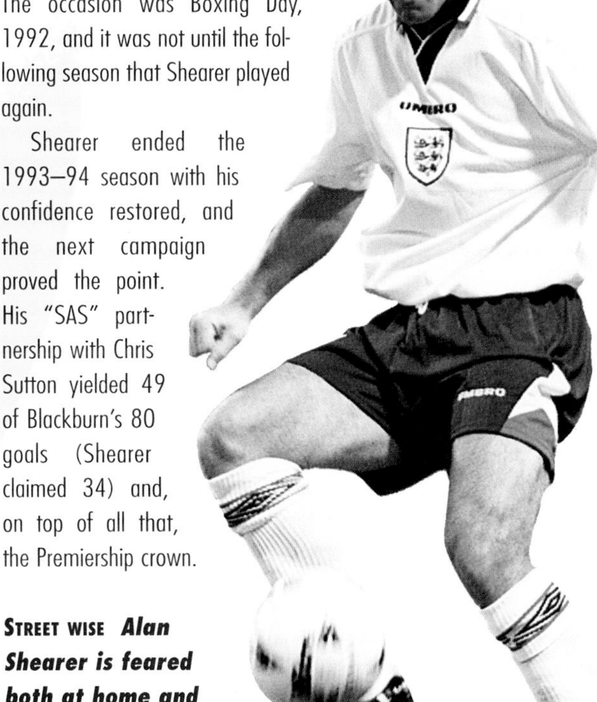

STREET WISE ***Alan Shearer is feared both at home and abroad***

Alan Shearer – England	
Position:	*Striker*
Born:	*Newcastle, August 13, 1970*
Clubs:	*Southampton, Blackburn Rovers*
Debut:	*vs. France, 1992*

"When it comes to finishing, his strength is that he's got no obvious weaknesses."

Terry Venables, England coach.

ALAN SHEARER

TOMAS SKUHRAVY

Czech spearhead

Tomas Skuhravy was one of the most effective attackers at the 1990 World Cup finals – netting a hat-trick against the USA – and appeared poised for further glory.

Indeed, had it not been for Toto Schillaci's penalty in Italy's Third Place Play-off victory against England, Skuhravy would have shared five-goal billing as the event's top scorer.

Instead, the smiling giant had to settle for second place in the scorers' chart and the consolation of a lucrative three-year contract with Italian club Genoa. Successive contract extensions kept Skuhravy happy – until the club was relegated in 1995.

There was little prospect of Skuhravy remaining in Genoa and, in the middle of the following season, he was loaned to Sporting Clube of Portugal. Skuhravy felt that a transfer was essential in order for him to secure his place spearheading the Czech Republic's attack for Euro96™, but the deal collapsed and he returned to Italy.

CAPITAL GAINS

Skuhravy was brought up in the village of Nymburk, some 20 miles from Prague. At 13, he began playing for a local team, Prerov Nad Labem, and, at 16, he was snapped up by Sparta, big-city giants and the greatest club in the country.

One year later, coach Josef Jarabinsky pushed him into the first team and, in the seven seasons which followed, Skuhravy ran up 76 league goals in just over 200 games. It was an ideal pedigree to earn a move to Italy yet, for Skuhravy, the main attraction of Italy was neither football nor financial. It was the lure of Ferrari.

As the son of a mechanic, Skuhravy had always had a passion for cars and the prestige Italian marque in particular. He once said his ambition had been to be a Formula One racing driver rather than footballer.

PROVING DOUBTERS WRONG

Skuhravy never expected the success which came his way and changed his life and career in 1990. He says: "Looking back now, it all seems like a dream. The satisfaction was not so much having scored the goals but having proved so many people wrong. Seven or eight sports writers back home didn't think I should have been in the squad let alone the team!"

Now, leading the attack of the newly-independent Czech Republic into the finals of a major tournament for the first time in their short history, Skuhravy has it all to prove again. But he knows all about proving the doubters wrong.

IDEAL FORMULA ***Tomas Skuhravy is a danger in the air and on the ground***

Tomas Skuhravy – Czech Republic

POSITION:	*Striker*
BORN:	*Nymburk, September 7, 1965*
CLUBS:	*Sparta Prague, Genoa (Italy), Sporting Clube (Portugal), Genoa*
DEBUTS:	*Czechoslovakia, vs. Poland, 1985; Czech Republic, vs. Lithuania, 1994*

"I hope I have now proved my point that my game is about much more than merely heading the ball."

Tomas Skuhravy.

Portuguese link man

PAULO SOUSA

Paulo Manuel de Carvalho Sousa promises to become one of the biggest names at Euro96™, courtesy of his ability to both organize his team-mates in midfield and, simultaneously, stop the opposition.

Portugal will rely on Sousa, just as three of Europe's greatest clubs have learned to do over the last eight years. Marcello Lippi, coach of the Juventus team which Sousa helped to win the 1995 Italian league title, says: "Paulo is the classical deep-lying general. He is as important to his team in breaking down attacks as he is in organizing team-mates."

Sousa's abilities emerged in his home town of Viseu. As a schoolboy he wanted to become a teacher but as Sousa grew aware of his talent for football, so turning professional became more appealing.

BARGAIN BUY

A local youth team, Repesesc, were the first to benefit. He played centre-forward and no opponent could knock him off the ball. Sousa scored 12 goals in one match. A few months later, Benfica paid Repesesc £400 to take Sousa to Lisbon.

Nene, the former Portuguese international who had become Benfica's youth coach, encouraged Sousa to work at his game and he soon joined the Portuguese junior squad. A 1989 World Youth Cup-winner, he returned to find first-team coach Sven-Goran Eriksson throwing him in at the deep end, as playmaker.

His debut came in a friendly against Holland's PSV Eindhoven. A week later, Sousa's league debut was against cross-city rivals Belenenses — a match Sousa would long remember. He was selected for the post-match dope test, but he was so dehydrated from the match that it took him five hours before he could provide the necessary sample!

"Because he is powerful in the tackle he provides extra guarantees to protect his own defence and win the ball for his own attack."

Marcello Lippi, Juventus coach, describing Sousa's strength.

TWO-WAY HERO ***Paulo Sousa is a hero in Italy and Portugal***

MOVING ON

In 1992, Juventus first inquired about Sousa. Benfica ruled out any chance of a deal and did not tell him. Sousa, finding out from the media, was furious.

An administrative error meant Benfica failed to offer Sousa a new contract within the stipulated time so he became a free agent, able to negotiate a new deal anywhere, and it was Benfica's turn to be furious when Sousa signed for their greatest rivals, neighbours Sporting.

By the time FIFA had settled the legal wrangle between the clubs over the transfer fee, Sousa had secured a deal with Juventus and earned a reputation which powers ahead of him into Euro96™.

Paulo Manuel de Carvalho Sousa – Portugal

POSITION:	Midfield
BORN:	Viseu, August 30, 1970
CLUBS:	Benfica, Sporting Clube, Juventus (Italy)
DEBUT:	vs. Holland, 1992

HRISTO STOICHKOV

Dark, moody and magnificent

No one has greater confidence in the ability of Hristo Stoichkov to shred opposing defences than Stoichkov himself. The confidence is certainly not misplaced.

In the dour old 1960s and 1970s, the cult of the superstar represented by this product of Plovdiv was frowned upon. But Stoichkov personifies a political, social and sporting revolution and the fans love him for it. Without Stoichkov's enormous will to win, Bulgaria would never have recovered from the shock of their opening 3–0 defeat by Nigeria at the 1994 World Cup finals to reach the semi-finals and, ultimately, a best-ever fourth place.

Not for Stoichkov the quiet life. In his early days, he was banned *sine die* in Bulgaria after a cup final dust-up. The ban held for six months and was then lifted because the Bulgarian football federation feared the consequences of going to the 1986 World Cup finals without Stoichkov and several team-mates who had also been involved. In the end, they took him to Mexico, but he did not play.

BUMPY RIDE IN BARCELONA

Stoichkov's talents soon earned international renown and a transfer to Barcelona at the specific behest of their coach Johan Cruyff. Not that the two flamboyant men always saw eye-to-eye.

In 1992, Stoichkov caused consternation in Barcelona when he said, on the eve of the Champions Cup Final against Sampdoria at Wembley, that he was considering a lucrative offer from Italy's Napoli. Cruyff threatened to drop him from the Wembley line-up and Stoichkov decided, almost overnight, that Napoli was not for him.

But the lure of Italian football was never extinguished and Stoichkov's brilliance at USA '94 brought first the European Footballer of the Year accolade then a lucrative transfer from Catalonia to Parma.

LAYING FOUNDATIONS

Here, Stoichkov believes, he has laid the foundations on which to build the rest of his playing career – both with Parma and with Bulgaria's national team.

Stoichkov says: "In the national team we have a new mentality. A lot of it is to do with the fact that almost all our best players now play professionally in western Europe. This means the players can contribute so much more than before when it comes to discussing tactics before a match."

Stoichkov is a trend-setting footballer. He has led Bulgaria into the European finals for the first time and he is their second-top scorer. He ended the Euro96™ qualifiers with 29 goals, 18 fewer than 1970s' star Hristo Bonev.

By the end of Euro96™, Stoichkov will probably have narrowed the gap.

SPEAKING OUT ***Hristo Stoichkov both plays and talks a good match***

Hristo Stoichkov – Bulgaria	
POSITION:	Forward
BORN:	Plovdiv, February 8, 1966
CLUBS:	Barcelona (Spain), Parma (Italy)
DEBUT:	vs. Belgium, 1987

"Stoichkov is capable of producing the unexpected in every game." Dimitar Penev, Bulgarian coach.

ANDONI ZUBIZARRETA

Vintage stuff

Goalkeepers are frequently compared with wine – they improve with age – by which standard Spain's No. 1 Andoni Zubizarreta is vintage stuff. He has made more than 100 international appearances for his country, and he's not finished yet!

Now, 10 years after becoming the world's first £1 million goalkeeper and two years after being given away hastily by Barcelona, Zubizarreta remains not merely Spain's No. 1, but among the best in Europe.

"Zubi" benefited from learning his trade in an ideal football environment – the Basque country of northern Spain which has a matchless tradition for producing outstanding goalkeepers. In the 1950s, at Athletic Bilbao, there was Carmelo Cedrun; in the 1960s, at Real Sociedad, there was Jose Araquistain; then Bilbao discovered Jose Angel Iribar; Sociedad provided his successor as national team keeper and captain in Luis Arconada. Local-born rivals such as Javier Urruti and Pedro Artola left to find fame and fortune with Barcelona.

Zubizarreta has been, perhaps, the best of all. He began with second division Alaves, was spotted by Bilbao and thrown into the first division hurly-burly, at 22.

Keeping with tradition

He was outstanding as Bilbao won first the league then the league-and-cup double. He played for the Spanish team beaten by England in the 1984 European Under-21 Championship Final and, a year later, made his senior debut as substitute for Arconada in a 3–1 win over Finland. Months later, he was awarded the Zamora Trophy – named after Spain's great goalkeeper of pre-war days – as the top goalkeeper in the league and, in 1986, he was the subject of a world record transfer.

Barcelona paid Bilbao £1.2 million, the highest ever for a goalkeeper, to buy Zubizarreta two days before the club's appearance in the European Champions Cup Final against Steaua Bucharest. Zubizarreta was ineligible, the deadline having long passed, so he could only watch as the Catalan giants, coached by Terry Venables, were beaten on penalties after a stifling goalless draw.

RECORD BREAKER **_Zubizaretta has played in more than 100 international matches_**

Capping it all

Soon, however, he was repaying Barcelona for their faith and for the fabulous eight-year contract. In the 1994 World Cup qualifiers, he overtook Jose Camacho's record of 81 caps for Spain and he has defied all challengers to his job.

In the summer of 1994 Barcelona, seeking scapegoats for their 4–0 thrashing by Milan in the Champions Cup Final, turned on Zubizarreta and he joined Valencia on virtually a free transfer.

Valencia have been delighted with Zubizarreta's form. So has the rest of Spain.

Andoni Zubizarreta – Spain

Position:	*Goalkeeper*
Born:	*Bilbao, October 23, 1961*
Clubs:	*Alaves, Athletic Bilbao, Barcelona, Valencia*
Debut:	*vs. Finland, 1985*

"I will go on as many seasons as I feel up to it. As long as the national coach needs me, then I will be there." Andoni Zubizarreta.

GUIDE TO THE COUNTRIES

The European Championship is the continent's most important exclusive international event in football. Indeed, qualifying for the recent Euro finals had been considered harder than qualification for the World Cup, until the tournament expanded to 16 nations for Euro96™.

Here is how the "big fish" and the "minnows" – 47 nations playing 241 matches in 20 months – thrashed it out for 15 of them to join hosts England in contesting the finals of Euro96™.

GROUP 1

Romania maintained the status earned by their quarter-final achievement at the 1994 World Cup, while France took revenge over Israel – against whom they had lost a crucial World Cup qualifying tie in 1993. The only upset the Romanians suffered was in losing their penultimate match by 3–1 at home to the French. Azerbaijan collected their only point with a draw against disappointing Poland.

	P	W	D	L	F	A	Pts
Romania	10	6	3	1	18	9	21
France	10	5	5	0	22	2	20
Slovakia	10	4	2	4	14	18	14
Poland	10	3	4	3	14	12	13
Israel	10	3	3	4	13	13	12
Azerbaijan	10	0	1	9	2	29	1

GROUP 2

Spain qualified easily, but holders Denmark found it tough after drawing away to Macedonia and losing to Spain in their opening three games. Belgium were a major disappointment, failing to take advantage of Denmark's lapses. Macedonia's tournament debut was marred by crowd trouble which incurred a two-match home game ban.

	P	W	D	L	F	A	Pts
Spain	10	8	2	0	25	4	26
Denmark	10	6	3	1	19	9	21
Belgium	10	4	3	3	17	13	15
Macedonia	10	1	4	5	9	18	7
Cyprus	10	1	4	5	6	20	7
Armenia	10	1	2	7	5	17	5

GROUP 3

Switzerland and Turkey dominated the only five-nation qualifying group. Switzerland ended their campaign winning qualification, but losing manager Roy Hodgson, while Turkey led for much of the way and thus reached the finals for the first time. Sweden, third in the 1994 World Cup, fell away badly after star forward Tomas Brolin broke an ankle in an early group win over Hungary.

	P	W	D	L	F	A	Pts
Switzerland	8	5	2	1	15	7	17
Turkey	8	4	3	1	16	8	15
Sweden	8	2	3	3	9	10	9
Hungary	8	2	2	4	7	13	8
Iceland	8	1	2	5	3	12	5

GROUP 4

Italian observers believed they had been offered an easy ride to the finals, and that Ukraine were the only rivals who offered any threat. Wrong on both counts. Italy lost their first home match by 2–1 against Croatia – the surprise team of the entire qualifying tournament – while Ukraine were never in the running . Estonia and San Marino (in Group Eight) were the only nations to lose all their qualifying matches.

	P	W	D	L	F	A	Pts
Croatia	10	7	2	1	22	5	23
Italy	10	7	2	1	20	6	23
Lithuania	10	5	1	4	13	12	16
Ukraine	10	4	1	5	11	15	13
Slovenia	10	3	2	5	13	13	11
Estonia	10	0	0	10	3	31	0

Group 5

The outcome of this group was not determined until the last day when Holland beat group leaders Norway, 3–0, to drop them to third place and out of the qualification picture. The Czech Republic, competing under their new guise for the time, were group winners. Holland left it late and their narrow "survival" was reflected in their having to go into the qualifying play-off. All Luxembourg's goals came in 1–0 victories.

	P	W	D	L	F	A	Pts
Czech Republic	10	6	3	1	21	6	21
Holland	10	6	2	2	23	5	20
Norway	10	6	2	2	17	7	20
Belarus	10	3	2	5	8	13	11
Luxembourg	10	3	1	6	3	21	10
Malta	10	0	2	8	2	22	2

Group 6

Portugal were hailed as one of Europe's finest young teams after their 3–0 win over the Republic of Ireland in Lisbon. Austria might have qualified, but lost their chance in an eight-goal thriller against Northern Ireland on the last match day. The Republic of Ireland sneaked into a qualifying play-off against Holland, despite their goalless draw with Liechtenstein, whose one goal scored and 40 conceded were the worst records in the entire qualifying event.

	P	W	D	L	F	A	Pts
Portugal	10	7	2	1	29	7	23
Rep. of Ireland	10	5	2	3	17	11	17
N. Ireland	10	5	2	3	20	15	17
Austria	10	5	1	4	29	14	16
Latvia	10	4	0	6	11	20	12
Liechtenstein	10	0	1	9	1	40	1

Group 7

History appeared to be repeating itself midway through the group when Bulgaria, who had beaten Germany in the 1994 World Cup quarter-finals, defeated them 3–2 in Sofia. But no one else raised much serious opposition in the group. Germany, surprisingly held 1–1 at home by Wales, ultimately topped the table. Wales made the wrong sort of history by allowing Moldova to open their competitive international history with a 3–2 victory in Chisinau.

	P	W	D	L	F	A	Pts
Germany	10	8	1	1	27	10	25
Bulgaria	10	7	1	2	24	10	22
Georgia	10	5	0	5	14	13	15
Moldova	10	3	0	7	11	27	9
Wales	10	2	2	6	9	19	8
Albania	10	2	2	6	10	16	8

Group 8

Russia were, along with Spain and France, the only nations to end the qualifying series unbeaten. They, also like Spain, dropped only four points during the qualifying competition. Scotland cruised through in second place. Greece won their first four games, but lost the next three and, after 20 games, Finland led the group. San Marino lost every game, the Faroe Islands eight, and each one was by at least two goals.

Group winners were guaranteed qualification. The tie-breaker for two teams finishing on the same number of points began with the results between them – not goal difference.

	P	W	D	L	F	A	Pts
Russia	10	8	2	0	34	5	26
Scotland	10	7	2	1	19	3	23
Greece	10	6	0	4	23	9	18
Finland	10	5	0	5	18	18	15
Faroe Islands	10	2	0	8	10	35	6
San Marino	10	0	0	10	2	36	0

The Qualifying Play-off

Six group runners-up qualified by right – the other two played off for the 16th and final place at Euro96™. The final placings for these teams were decided by their record against the first, third and fourth in each group, so only when the final whistle went in the very last qualifying game could this table be compiled and it came out as follows:

Country (Group)	P	W	D	L	F	A	Pts
Italy (4)	6	4	1	1	12	4	13
Bulgaria (7)	6	4	0	2	14	8	12
Scotland (8)	6	3	2	1	5	2	11
Turkey (3)	6	3	2	1	10	8	11
Denmark (2)	6	3	2	1	9	7	11
France (1)	6	2	4	0	8	2	10
Holland (5)	6	2	2	2	6	5	8
Rep. of Ire (6)	6	2	1	3	8	10	7

Holland 2, Republic of Ireland 0
December 13, 1995 (Anfield)

The play-off venue favoured Jack Charlton's Irish team, because of their greater support. However, Holland defied not only Ireland's supporters, but their footballers too, and won 2–0 in superb style. Patrick Kluivert was the hero, scoring both goals, the second in the final minute of the second half.

ENGLAND EXPECTS ...

ENGLAND

EURO96™ HOSTS

GROUP A

Host nations are in a deceptive position. Playing at home, in front of their own fans, in familiar surroundings, is an undoubted advantage. But England coach Terry Venables and his players are also distinctly aware of the challenges thrown across their ambition of winning the European Championship for the first time. And an extra challenge facing Venables and England is the level of expectation of home fans.

The very fervour and support of a home crowd brings extra pressures which can affect a team performance. The last time England staged a major event, the 1966 World Cup, it took a solo effort from Bobby Charlton in their second match – against Mexico – to break down the wall of nervous tension.

Host nations in all major championships encounter problems in finding suitable opposition against whom to plan and prepare. As UEFA now embraces 49 member nations, that meant an extraordinarily busy qualifying competition and very few European nations had dates free to play friendly matches – they were too involved trying to reach England the hard way!

THE WEIGHT OF TRADITION

The organized modern game of association football was conceived in England in the middle of the nineteenth century, the first formal laws were drawn up in 1863, the first national competition (the FA Cup) founded in 1871, the first league championship in 1888. Such historical pre-eminence was matched for many years by England's international results. It was not until 1953 that England were defeated on home soil by continental opposition – by Ferenc Puskas's legendary Hungarians. Yet, just 13 years later, England won the World Cup as hosts.

But this weight of history has proved a burden beyond a succession of England managers and players. England's international record has not matched that of clubs in European competition. Since 1970, England have failed to earn even qualification for three of six World Cup finals and two of six European finals. In fact, England have won just one of their last nine games in the European Championships finals.

IN THE HOT-SEAT

Following England's failure to qualify for the World Cup finals in 1994, manager Graham Taylor was replaced by Terry Venables, a highly regarded coach. Unlike his predecessors, Venables did not have to worry about a qualifying competition, but it worked against him as he could not blood new players in the competitive arena.

Venables immediately set to work building not only a football team but a support team of coaches who could bring to the challenge a wealth of big-occasion experience – such as veteran international aide Don Howe and younger coaches such as Middlesbrough manager Bryan Robson.

The nucleus of his England team soon became apparent in a series of friendlies plus the 1995 Umbro Cup tournament involving the varied styles of opposition provided by Japan, Sweden and World Cup-holders Brazil.

YOUNG LIONS

Arsenal goalkeeper David Seaman and centre-back team-mate Tony Adams have been consistent selections within the Venables defensive unit with captain David Platt – a veteran of continental football through his years in Italy with Bari, Juventus and Sampdoria – foraging out of midfield. Blackburn Rovers' Alan Shearer has led the attack with the likes of Nick Barmby, Peter Beardsley, Les Ferdinand and Teddy Sheringham as raiding partners.

However, the undoubted jewel in England's crown is midfielder Paul

EURO FACT ***England's first match in the European Championship was (Sir) Alf Ramsey's first as manager. It was played at Hillsborough, Sheffield, on October 3, 1962. England drew 1–1 with France, but lost the return 5–2. Only Ray Wilson and Bobby Moore kept their places in the team to win the World Cup four years later.***

Diamond in the rough ***Paul Gascoigne's health, physical and emotional, will be vital to England***

Gascoigne, a player whose talents are brilliant but whose body is fragile. A knee injury in 1991 and a broken leg in 1994 both led to one-year absences and each was followed by an international transfer – from Tottenham to Italians Lazio in 1992 and from Lazio to Scottish giants Rangers in 1995. If – and this is a big if – Gascoigne can keep fit in the run-up to and during Euro96™, England will be a much feared force.

England's low position in the FIFA World Rankings has been the result of the nation's inability to qualify for the 1994 World Cup. Results in friendlies since Venables took over have seen a slight improvement, but England needs to have success in competitive matches to rise significantly in the eyes of the world. Venables has never ceased to praise the depth of young talent emerging in the English game. But he has also kept his feet on the ground. That has meant, more than once, reminding the more impatient well-wishers that youth must be balanced by experience if England are, finally, to become champions of Europe.

European Championship Record

1960	did not enter
1964	First round
1968	3rd place
1972	Quarter-final
1976	did not qualify
1980	Group round
1984	did not qualify
1988	Group round
1992	Group round

Terry Venables

Born January 6, 1943. Venables was the first England player to appear at all international levels. A midfield general, his playing career spanned 15 years from joining Chelsea in 1960, through spells with Tottenham Hotspur, Queens Park Rangers and Crystal Palace, before he devoted himself full-time to coaching. His work with Palace helped earn him one of the world's plum jobs with Barcelona where he won the Spanish championship before returning to Tottenham as manager, then managing director. Venables left White Hart Lane in 1993 and was appointed to succeed Graham Taylor as England coach at the start of the following year.

ENGLAND

Brains trust ***Terry Venables (centre) flanked by assistants Bryan Robson (left) and Don Howe***

"If this had been a qualifying match, nobody would have complained."

Terry Venables, England coach answering criticism of a 0–0 friendly draw away to Norway.

SWITZERLAND

REGULAR AS CLOCKWORK

Euro96™ Group 3 Winners

Group A

New leader ***Artur Jorge takes over where Roy Hodgson left off***

Switzerland have re-emerged as an international force in the 1990s. Much of the credit goes to Englishman Roy Hodgson, whose managerial talents brought the Swiss to the last World Cup finals – for the first time in 28 years – and now to a debut at the European Championship finals.

However, Hodgson will not be in charge when Switzerland appear in the opening match of Euro96™ against England at Wembley on June 8. In November 1995, he accepted a lucrative offer to coach Italian giants Internazionale, so Switzerland had to find a new boss. The man they found was another non-Swiss national, Artur Jorge from Portugal. He appeared ideally qualified to pick up the baton, having coached FC Porto to success in the 1987 European Champions Cup.

Hodgson maintained a settled side, with strong organization based around a sweeper (usually Alain Geiger) in defence and two up front – one of them the outstanding Stephane Chapuisat. Yet Switzerland remained a team in the best traditions of the word, proving it by securing qualification despite Chapuisat's absence through long-term injury. In the 1994 World Cup they surprised Scotland, Portugal and Italy in their qualifying group; in the European Championship, they ended two points clear of fellow qualifiers Turkey and a Swedish side fresh from their third-place achievement at USA '94.

Cultures club

Regional differences, not only in language and philosophy, but also in football styles, have caused every succeeding managers problems since Karl Rappan took Switzerland to the World Cup quarter-finals in 1930s. The trick has been to find a method and tactic which suits players from French, Italian and German backgrounds.

Hodgson and Jorge have been fortunate in that the basic talent of the current generation of Swiss players is so high and that they have been exposed to the different cultures of club football around Europe. Switzerland's threat remains built on foundations provided by their German-based exports such as Bayern Munich's Ciri Sforza in midfield, Borussia Dortmund's Chapuisat – assuming he regains fitness – and Freiburg winger Alain Sutter.

Experienced captain Alan Geiger, with more than 100 international caps, holds the defence together while Servette's Marco Pascolo has emerged as undisputed No 1 goalkeeper. Manchester United fans may remember another of the Swiss stars, Kubilay Turkyilmaz, one of the Galatasaray players who wrecked the Reds' Champions Cup ambitions in 1994.

Early qualification

Switzerland, officially, were the fourth nation certain of a place in the finals of the European Championship after hosts England and runaway qualifying leaders Spain and Russia. Their record against Turkey, Sweden and Hungary in the five-team group meant that even if Switzerland had finished second behind Turkey, they could not become one of the two "worst runners-up" who played off for the last remaining slot.

Until recently, Switzerland in football terms has meant action in committee rooms rather than out on the pitch. Yet the Swiss were not only importers of football they were also enthusiastic exporters. Their football missionaries played very significant roles in the rapid development of the game in northern Italy, and it was a Swiss, Hans Gamper, who founded the Spanish giants, Barcelona.

EURO FACT ***Switzerland's first-ever match in the European Championship was a 3–1 defeat by Holland – who will be among their first-round group rivals at Euro96™.***

"We let ourselves down a little, the way we went out of the last World Cup. We want to improve on that." *Alain Geiger, Swiss captain.*

The oldest surviving club is St Gallen, but current champions Grasshopper-Club of Zurich are probably the best-known. They were founded by the English in 1886, though their neighbours, FC Zurich, have probably achieved more in Europe with two Champions Cup semi-final appearances to their credit.

Scores to settle

Switzerland, one of FIFA's founding members, were one of three candidates bidding for the rights to host the 1998 World Cup finals. Their bid was buried in peremptory fashion: FIFA's executive committee ruled it out of order since it involved the use of temporary stands to increase the capacity of the stadia – forbidden since the Bastia Stadium Disaster in France in 1992. The hosting vote went to France, so getting there will be the Swiss priority once they have settled a couple of scores with England.

The last time Switzerland came to England for a major championship finals, West Germany beat them 5–0 in their World Cup opener and they failed to progress beyond the first round. Then, in November 1995, they were beaten 3–1 by the Euro96™ hosts in a friendly. This time, they say, things will be different.

European Championship Record

1960	did not enter
1964	Second round
1968	did not qualify
1972	did not qualify
1976	did not qualify
1980	did not qualify
1984	did not qualify
1988	did not qualify
1992	did not qualify

Artur Jorge

Born on February 13, 1946, Jorge – a former Portuguese international centre-forward – played for FC Porto, Academica Coimbra, Benfica and Belenenses before retiring at 31 because of a broken leg. After obtaining a doctorate in German at the University of Coimbra, he graduated from the East German sports coaching academy in Leipzig. Jorge coached Porto to Champions Cup success in 1987 and later guided Paris Saint-Germain to the French championships before returning to Portugal with Benfica.

OUT FOR REVENGE ***Switzerland, beaten by England last November, intend turning the tables on June 8***

SWITZERLAND

HOLLAND

EURO96™ GROUP 5 RUNNERS-UP
(BEAT THE REPUBLIC OF IRELAND IN A PLAY-OFF)

GROUP A

QUICK FIRE ***Edgar Davids shoots past Paul McGrath***

In their qualifying play-off against the Republic of Ireland, at Liverpool, Dutch fans may have been outnumbered but they had history was on their side. Their team had won the European Championship in 1988 – beating the Republic to qualify for the semi-final – and overcome the Irish again at the 1994 World Cup finals in Orlando.

The 2–0 victory, in December 1995, courtesy of goals from Patrick Kluivert, turned Holland from late-comers to the party into one of the top tips for the title. But, to justify that status, the Dutch must ensure they are not their own worst enemies. Too often they have entered major championships concerned more with their own internal political wrangles than with the opposition out on the pitch.

TIFFS AND TANTRUMS

It took Johan Cruyff's persuasion to stop Marco Van Basten walking out on the ultimately triumphant European Championship squad in 1988; before the 1990 World Cup, player power forced the dismissal of coach Thys Libregts and then the players still were not happy with his replacement, Leo Beenhakker.

Again, before the last World Cup a great deal of time and concern was wasted on the rift between national coach Dick Advocaat and veteran Ruud Gullit, a squabble complicated by the bizarre events of December 1993, when Barcelona coach Cruyff turned down the opportunity to take up the part-time appointment to manage Holland at USA '94.

> **EURO FACT** *Holland's best finish in the European Championship, prior to 1988, was in 1976 when they beat hosts Yugoslavia 3–2 after extra time in the third-place play-off.*

Holland reached the quarter-finals before going down to eventual World Cup-winners Brazil. Now, they have a new manager in Guus Hiddink and a new-look team following the retirements of Frank Rijkaard (from all football) and Ronald Koeman (from the international game).

DOING IT THE HARD WAY

Hans Van Breukelen, goalkeeper when Holland won the European crown in 1988, always said that his country made a habit of qualifying the hard way – and his comments were borne out by events in 1994 and 1995. In their final qualifying game, Holland beat Norway 3–0, and leapt up from third in the group to second, behind the Czech Republic, with the Norwegians – group leaders going into the match – third.

The Dutch national team has often suffered from a philosophical dispute over whether they should rely on the individual talent available at the Big Three – Ajax, PSV Eindhoven and Feyenoord – or whether to commit themselves to doing things the Ajax way.

Coach Hiddink, who took over from PSV-bound Dick Advocaat in the middle of the qualifying campaign, tried both formulae. The first did not work well and it was only after Hiddink committed himself to the Ajax module, against Norway in Rotterdam, that Holland stepped up a gear. Against the Republic of Ireland at Anfield, Hiddink called on eight current and two former Ajax players in his starting line-up – even using Ajax's Winston Bogarde in place of suspended club-mate Frank de Boer.

TOTAL FOOTBALL

The depth of quality consistently available has been beyond dispute ever since Dutch clubs such as Feyenoord first made their mark in the European Champions Cup in the early 1960s. Feyenoord, in 1970, became the first Dutch club to win the event, and Ajax followed up immediately with their 1971–73 hat-trick.

This was the revolutionary era of "total football," a style in which players of high technical and tactical ability were able to inter-change at a speed and with a facility which confused almost everyone they played – until the bubble burst with Holland's 2–1 defeat by West Germany in the 1974 World Cup Final.

Dutch confidence in their own ability and methods was unshaken. Ajax are now one of only three clubs – Juventus and Barcelona are the others – to have won all three European club competitions. Their enlightened youth development policies made headlines around the world after Ajax dominated 1995 by winning first the Champions League Cup then the World Club Cup. Holland may be considered better placed than most other countries in terms of natural talent with Edwin van der Sar in goal, Danny Blind in central defence, Clarence Seedorf, Ronald de Boer and Edgar Davids in midfield and Kluivert up front.

No wonder Holland are one of the favourites to win Euro96™.

European Championship Record

1960	did not enter
1964	Second round
1968	did not qualify
1972	did not qualify
1976	3rd place
1980	Finals Group
1984	did not qualify
1988	Champions
1992	Semi-finalists

Guus Hiddink

Born on November 8, 1946, Hiddink played in the 1960s and 1970s for his home-town club Sport Varsseveld then De Graafschap, PSV Eindhoven and NEC Nijmegen before moving into the NASL with Washington Diplomats and San Jose Earthquakes. He returned to Holland and coached De Graafschap and then PSV where he took over as senior coach in 1986. In 1988, he coached PSV to a European Champions Cup victory before moving to Spain with Valencia. Hiddink succeeded Dick Advocaat as national coach at the end of 1994.

FOR CLUB AND COUNTRY ***Holland, with a nucleus of Ajax players, line-up for the playoff against Ireland***

"We will be confident but not over-confident. That is a mistake we've made too often in the past." *Danny Blind, Dutch defender.*

CELTIC PRIDE

SCOTLAND

EURO96™ GROUP 8 RUNNERS-UP

GROUP A

An easy 5–0 win over San Marino in Glasgow in November 1995 provided confirmation that Scotland will be appearing at the finals of the European Championship for the second time in succession – and the second time ever.

Goals from Aberdeen pair of Eoin Jess and Scott Booth, others from Ally McCoist and Pat Nevin and a Fabio Francini own goal meant "mission accomplished" for former college lecturer, coach Craig Brown

GLORIOUS HISTORY

Such an achievement might be considered long overdue, given Scotland's football history. After all, they hosted the first ever international match, a 0–0 draw against England in 1872. Scotland have also produced two of the most famous clubs in the world in Rangers and Celtic as well as outstanding individual talents ranging from Alex James in the 1920s and 1930s to George Young in the 1950s, Jim Baxter and Dave Mackay and Denis Law in the 1960s, Kenny Dalglish in the 1970s and 1980s and Paul McStay and Ally McCoist in recent years.

Scotland's general international path matched that of England. They began together, quit FIFA together in the 1920s, then returned simultaneously to the FIFA fold in 1946. The Scots should also have travelled to the 1950 World Cup finals in Brazil. The now-defunct Home International Championship – featuring Scotland, England, Northern Ireland and Wales – was used as the qualifying event and the top two teams were guaranteed places at the finals. Scotland insisted they would go only if they ended up top of the group. In the event England were top and Scotland, having finished second, opted to stay at home.

Scotland's previously poor record in the European Championship is in stark contrast to the World Cup, where the Scots were finalists at five consecutive tournaments between 1974 and 1990.

TWO FINALS APPEARANCES

Brown's niche in domestic football history is to have shared in plotting two European finals campaigns – the first, in 1992, as assistant to Andy Roxburgh. Holland and Germany were too strong for the Scots, but they gained a degree of consolation with a 3–0 triumph over the CIS.

The 1994 World Cup qualifying competition challenge in a difficult group foundered on home draws and away defeats against Switzerland, Italy and Portugal, but that is now a matter for historical regret after victory over the Sammarinese minnows handed Scotland a second-place finish in Group Eight behind Russia and guaranteed them a spot at Euro96™ one of the six runners-up with the best comparative records.

MAN IN COMMAND
Scotland and Leeds midfield general Gary McAllister is a dead-ball specialist

Brown admitted: "After failing to get to the World Cup finals in the United States it would have been pretty depressing to miss out on successive finals. But we have come through the section losing only once and conceding just three goals in the group. Now we want to make significant progress. Scottish football has been much maligned recently

EURO FACT *Scotland received a special fair play award at the 1992 European Championship finals for the behaviour of their "tartan army" of fans.*

but both the under-21s, in their own European competition, and the senior team have qualified. We're not sparkling but we are efficient."

Significant progress means that Scotland must advance beyond the first round of any major finals event for the first time in their history. Until now they have never escaped the group section in either World Cup or European Championship.

Comfortable qualification

Different times, different decisions. Scotland finished runners-up to Russia in their recent Euro96™ qualifying group but there was no question of them staying away from the finals. Indeed, they could be proud of their record. They drew both home and away against the Russians and lost only once, away to Greece. Brown's men ended up on 23 points – a total exceeded, across the qualifying board, by only Germany, Spain and, of course, Russia.

The draw for the finals at Birmingham brought an early Christmas present to all Scottish football fans – the chance to upset "the auld enemy" England in Group A at Wembley on June 15.

Brown will enter Euro96™ confident of causing an upset or two. His squad is a blend of young players such as Jess, Booth and John Collins, mixing well with veterans McCoist, reborn goalkeeper Jim Leighton and Nevin.

European Championship Record

1960	did not enter
1964	did not enter
1968	did not qualify
1972	did not qualify
1976	did not qualify
1980	did not qualify
1984	did not qualify
1988	did not qualify
1992	Group round

Craig Brown

Born on July 1, 1940. A schoolboy, youth and junior international, he played his club football with Rangers, Dundee – winning the Scottish championship in 1962 – and Falkirk. Knee trouble brought a premature end to his playing career. Brown became a primary school head teacher and then lecturer in primary education before returning to football in 1974 as assistant manager at Motherwell. He managed Clyde between 1977 and 1986 before becoming assistant national and under-21 coach. He succeeded Andy Roxburgh as national team manager and technical director in November 1993.

On the brink ***Scotland line up before their 5–0 qualifying round defeat of San Marino***

"We will not travel south simply to make up the numbers. We want to make an impact on the finals." *Craig Brown, Scotland coach.*

SPAIN

EURO96™ GROUP 2 WINNERS

GROUP B

Spain, despite an image of football dominated by the exploits and rivalry of Real Madrid and Barcelona, have a proud record in the European Championship.

Spain were the second winners, as hosts, in 1964, lost in the Final 20 years later, and have reached the finals tournament on two other occasions. As quarter-finalists at the last World Cup, two years ago, and one of the first qualifiers for England, they possess the pedigree of potential champions. Not that coach Javier Clemente would ever be heard boasting about his team's prospects. A down-to-earth Basque, Clemente learned from a promising playing career cut short early by serious injury, never to take anything for granted.

EURO FACT ***In 1959, on political grounds, Spain pulled out of the quarter-finals of the inaugural European Championship rather than play the Soviet Union – the eventual champions.***

TRULY NATIONAL TEAM

Accordingly Clemente has built a team which owes allegiance to neither Madrid nor Barcelona, but to the totality of the skill and power to be found in weekly Spanish league football. The success of that approach was evident at USA '94, where Spain might well have beaten Italy in the quarter-finals had veteran spearhead Julio Salinas not squandered a late open-goal opportunity.

Since then Clemente has continued to fine-tune his squad, maintaining faith in veteran Andoni Zubizarreta in goal, Barcelona's Miguel Angel Nadal in the centre of defence and offering a permanent attacking role out of midfield to the much-coveted Bilbao skipper, Julen Guerrero. Argentine-born Juan Antonio Pizzi – whose international form persuaded Barcelona to buy him from Tenerife – and Atletico Madrid midfielder Jose Caminero add to the attacking prowess.

GREAT TRADITION

Basque pragmatism has always been an important force within Spanish football. In 1950, Spain achieved their best World Cup finish of fourth place thanks in part to the aerial talents of the Athletic Bilbao centre-forward Telmo Zarra.

GREAT EXPECTATIONS ***The Spanish team line-up before their 4–1 victory over Belgium in Brussels***

PRIDE AND PRAGMATISM

> **"It is time we did ourselves justice in the big events."** *Javier Clemente, National coach of Spain.*

Any questions ***Coach Javier Clemente's press conference after Spain's 1–1 draw in Denmark***

International achievements over the next decade became the prerogative of Spain's clubs. Real Madrid, inspired by the great Argentine Alfredo Di Stefano and Hungarian Ferenc Puskas, won the European Champions' Cup in each of its first five years.

In that period Barcelona – with Hungarian genius of their own in Ladislav Kubala, Sandor Kocsis and Zoltan Czibor – twice won the Inter-Cities Fairs Cup (precursor of the UEFA Cup). Valencia, Atletico Madrid and Real Zaragoza joined successfully in the trophy hunting. But so many foreigners flooded into the Spanish league that the federation decided to shut the borders to give the national team a chance. Victory in the European Championship Final of 1964 was the reward, with a team guided in midfield by Luis Suarez.

Spain next reached the finals in 1980 but were eliminated at the group stage after losing their last match 2–1 to England. Four years later, however, they finished runners-up to France – defeating West Germany in the group section and then scoring a penalty shoot-out victory over Denmark in the semi-finals. Spain were finalists again in 1988, and again defeated Denmark – this time by 3–2 in the group stages – with goals from the Real Madrid trio of Michel, Emilio Butragueño and Rafael Gordillo. Successive defeats by Italy and West Germany ruled them out of further contention.

Bumpy Road to England

Clemente's campaign to reach Euro96™ began with a none-too-impressive 2–1 victory in Limassol in Cyprus in September 1994. The presence of the defending champions Denmark and Belgium in the group threatened trouble ahead. But Spain rose to the challenge. They won their first four games – including defeats of Denmark, 3–0 in Seville, and Belgium, 4–1 in Brussells – and, as early as Christmas 1994, they were favourites to top the group. Belgium took the first point from Spain, holding them 1–1 in Seville in March 1995, when Marc Degryse provided an instant retort to a 25th-minute goal from Guerrero.

But Spain were not to be shaken from their course. A draw, 1–1 away to Denmark in Copenhagen in mid-October, provided them with the single point which secured them top place in the group and a certain spot in the draw for the finals. Real Madrid midfielder Fernando Hierro converted a first-half penalty for the all-important goal.

Hierro is likely to be one of the most resolute of midfield specialists on duty at Euro96™. His long-striding, direct approach is a perfect foil for the youth of Guerrero and the guile of Caminero. In a strange reversal of history, Spain have become virtually a club side!

European Championship Record

1960	1st Round
1964	Champions
1968	Quarter-finalists
1972	1st Round
1976	Quarter-finalists
1980	Group Round
1984	Runners-up
1988	Group Round
1992	did not qualify

Javier Clemente

Born March 12, 1950. Clemente played for home-town Barakaldo as a teenager and joined Bilbao. A highly-promising midfield career was halted by injury at 24, but he joined the Athletic Bilbao coaching staff and quickly earned a reputation for producing effective, no-frills teams. Promoted to senior coach, he guided Bilbao to the Spanish league and cup double before taking unfashion-able Espanol Barcelona to the 1988 UEFA Cup Final. After a short spell with Atletico Madrid he was appointed national coach in the summer of 1990.

BULGARIA

EURO96™ GROUP 7 RUNNERS-UP

GROUP B

Bulgaria, after years of mediocrity revolutionized their football image with a remarkable campaign which took them to fourth place in the 1994 World Cup finals in the United States.

Previously, the Bulgarians had taken part in five World Cup finals and played 16 games without winning one. Almost overnight, Bulgaria became recognized as one of the most dangerous of opponents, a nation replete with star quality footballers such as forwards Hristo Stoichkov – 1994 European Footballer of the Year – and Emil Kostadinov and midfielders Yordan Lechkov and Krasimir Balakov.

All should be on duty at Euro96™ – a threat to anybody.

A CENTURY IN THE DOLDRUMS

Football has been played in Bulgaria for more than a century, interest having been aroused initially in 1884 by a British university team on a central European tour. The first Bulgarian football competition was not formed, however, until 1909 and the national federation only in 1923.

It was only after the Second World War – and the Communist takeover – that Bulgaria began to make international headway. After the regime took over in 1946, all the old sports organizations were dismantled and new clubs set up on a "state amateur" basis. Major industries and the armed services "sponsored" the new clubs and the army club CDNA (later CSKA) dominated the domestic game throughout the 1950s and 1960s.

That was the start of a slow, painful era of reconstruction within the Bulgarian game. The national team failed to qualify for the finals of both the 1988 and 1992 European Championships as well as for the 1990 World Cup. Much of the blame was later afforded to the fast-changing political situation which brought new sporting leaders to the fore and removed many of the financial and administrative privileges of clubs such as CSKA.

SUPER-POWERS OVERTHROWN

Signs that Bulgaria were ready to move forward came in the qualifying competition for the 1994 World Cup, when Bulgaria beat France, 2–1 in Paris, in the last minute of the last game to snatch a finals place out of the virtual grasp of their hosts. Bulgaria then defeated defending Cup-holders Germany 2–1 in the quarter-finals on the way to their fourth-place finish.

A further victory over the Germans came Bulgaria's way on the road to Euro96™ when they hit back from 1–0 down to triumph 3–2 in Sofia – goals which virtually secured the Bulgarians' first appearance in the finals of the European Championship.

Coach Dimitar Penev was a rock at the heart of Bulgaria's World Cup effort back in 1966, 1970 and 1974. But, unlike his managerial predecessors, Penev understands that progress at the World Cup depends on scoring goals as well as not conceding them.

EURO FACT ***Both current national coach Dimitar Penev and his predecessor, Ivan Vutsov, played in central defence for Bulgaria in their early – vain – European Championship qualifying campaigns in the 1960s.***

GETTING AHEAD ***Bulgarian striker Emil Kostadinov tackles German defender Markus Babbel***

The return to duty of Lubko Penev after illness means that Bulgaria could, if anything, be even more dangerous at Euro96™ than they were at the World Cup two years ago.

Otherwise fans at Elland Road, Leeds, and St James' Park, Newcastle, can expect to see a Bulgarian side with few changes in either tactics or personnel from the USA '94 version.

CONTINENTAL SHIFT

Borislav Mihailov was first choice as goalkeeper for the qualifying competition and will feel at home in England since he now plays his club football for Reading.

In front of him, Bulgaria maintain a close-marking defensive unit organised by sweeper Peter Hubchev. Hopefully, both he and balding midfielder Lechkov will have regained the form which appears to have deserted them at club level recently with SV Hamburg in Germany. Lechkov, certainly, was highly rated at the World Cup for the sheer class of his creative efforts wide on the right of midfield. Faced by Romania, France and Spain, the Bulgarians will need him at his inventive best.

The strike force will vary according to the state of each game and the strengths and weaknesses of the opposition. The fact that Stoichkov, Kostadinov, Nasko Sirakov and Lubko Penev can play up front or drop back towards midfield provides Bulgaria with vast possibilities for upsetting opposition tactics.

All that remains is for Bulgaria to maintain the confidence which complements their talent.

BERLIN WALL ***Bulgarian players stand to attention prior to their final qualifying match against Germany in Berlin, which they lost 3–1***

European Championship Record

1960	First round
1964	Second round
1968	Quarter-finalists
1972	did not qualify
1976	did not qualify
1980	did not qualify
1984	did not qualify
1988	did not qualify
1992	did not qualify

Dimitar Penev

Born on July 12, 1945. An outstanding defender in the 1960s and 1970s, he began playing with Lokomotiv Sofia and then won seven national championships and five cups with CSKA. He played 90 times for Bulgaria, including appearances at the World Cup finals in 1966, 1970 and 1974. After retiring he turned to coaching with CSKA, spent two years in Kuwait then returned to CSKA – whom he guided to five league titles and five cups. He was appointed national coach in succession to Ivan Vutsov in July 1991.

"Technically, we are much better than many more glamorous countries."

Hristo Stoichkov, Bulgarian striker.

ROMANIA

EURO96™ GROUP 1 WINNERS

GROUP B

Romania's players are on record as crediting the political revolution at the start of the 1990s as crucial to their recent success. The freedom to take their talents abroad helped them develop not only their skills but also their self-confidence as footballers.

The Romanians lost to Sweden in a penalty shoot-out at the quarter-final stage in the 1994 World Cup. Florin Raducioiu was their four-goal top scorer while Gheorghe Hagi scored three goals and created a majority of the rest.

World Cup stardom also brought recognition for coach Anghel Iordanescu, who was rewarded with promotion to the rank of General in the Romanian army. Iordanescu turned down a number of lucrative foreign offers to stay with the Romanian national team. Now he wants to see that loyalty rewarded in the European Championship.

Iordanescu says: "It's normal to see a downward curve in performance after a major competition. That's what happened to Denmark after they won the 1992 European Championship. It happened with us after the World Cup. Once you get that out of your system you come back all the better for the experience."

DECADES IN THE WILDERNESS

Romania were one of the few European teams to play in all of the first three World Cup finals (albeit unsuccessfully), but following the Communist takeover, their next finals appearance came at the 1970 World Cup. This was followed by another barren 14 years, when qualification for the 1984 European Championship was achieved.

By the time Romania returned to the World Cup finals, in 1990, the national coach was Mircea Lucescu, a star of the 1970 team. More importantly, the international profile of Romanian football had risen 100 per cent.

Steaua, the army club, had become, in 1986, the first eastern European team to win the Champions Cup. They defeated Barcelona in a penalty shoot-out after a 0–0 draw. Star players such as forward Marius Lacatus then led Romania into the second round of the 1990 World Cup finals.

By the time they got there, Romania had developed an even greater player in goal-scoring midfielder Gheorghe Hagi. He was not at his best in Italy but shone brightly at the 1994 World Cup finals and, at 31, may be considered at his peak for Euro96™.

ACE OF CLUBS

Steaua form the backbone of Romania's team, not surprisingly considering Iordanescu's past playing and managerial links with the record champions. As many as seven players who represented Steaua in the 1995–96 Champions League could see duty in England. These may include goalkeeper

EURO FACT ***Sweeper Miodrag Belodedici is one of only five players to have won the European Champions Cup with two separate clubs – Steaua Bucharest and Red Star Belgrade. The others are Frank Rijkaard, Dejan Savicevic, Ronald Koeman and Marcel Desailly.***

FINAL BOW ***Veteran Romania striker Marius Lacatus, in action during the defeat by France***

Bogdan Stelea, defenders Daniel Prodan, midfielder Constantin Galca and forwards Lacatus and Ion Vladoiu — to say nothing of "old boys" such as Hagi and sweeper Miodrag Belodedici.

FROSTY PRESS RECEPTION

Romania appeared likely to complete their qualifying campaign undefeated. Surprisingly, with a guaranteed Euro96™ place within reach, they lost 3–1 at home to France in their penultimate match. Media reaction was sharp and negative. It upset the players who had long been used to nothing more from their own press and broadcasters than unalloyed praise, and they vowed not to speak to the media.

This, of course, only heightened media speculation that Romania had lost their way, but the fears proved illusory. A 2–0 win away to Slovakia, with goals from Hagi and Dorinel Munteanu — perhaps Romania's top player in the qualifying competition — rounded off their campaign and left them top of the group.

The draw for the finals then offered the players an early chance of avenging that defeat by France with a meeting at St James' Park, Newcastle, on June 10.

European Championship Record

1960	Quarter-finalists
1964	First round
1968	did not qualify
1972	Quarter-finalists
1976	did not qualify
1980	did not qualify
1984	Group round
1988	did not qualify
1992	did not qualify

Anghel Iordanescu

Born on May 4, 1950. He succeeded Cornel Dinu in mid-1993 as national team coach after spending most of his long and successful career with Steaua Bucharest. As a player he was capped 64 times for the national team, scoring 26 goals, and won four national league titles with the club. He was both assistant coach and substitute player when Steaua beat Barcelona in the 1986 Champions Cup Final. Between 1990 and 1992 Iordanescu coached Cypriot team Anorthosis Famagusta before returning to Steaua in 1992. He was appointed national manager in 1993 and took Romania to the quarter-finals of the 1994 World Cup.

MOUNTING AMBITIONS ***Romania want to improve on the quarter-final showing at the last World Cup***

"From now on we will have nothing to say to the media. We are the ones who play the matches ... we do so for the honour of our country. Anyone who suggests otherwise is not worth consideration."

Gheorghe Hagi, Romanian star, following critical press reaction to the 3–1 home defeat by France in the qualifying round.

ROMANIA

FRANCE

THE COCKEREL CROWS AGAIN

EURO96™ GROUP 1 RUNNERS-UP

GROUP B

French manager Aime Jacquet and his players bear a responsibility not merely to their own ambition but to the nation and to the international game.

Players such as Christian Karembeu, Marcel Desailly and Didier Deschamps must wipe away bitter memories of the Marseille scandal and focus attention back on the integrity of the undoubted skills demonstrated over the years by players such as Raymond Kopa, Just Fontaine and Michel Platini.

The bribery scandal, which tarnished Marseille's achievement in becoming the first French club to win the European Champions Cup, was a sad conclusion to a remarkable decade, highlighted by the 1984 European Championship success. The joy of that night in 1993 quickly turned to misery as the club was banned from defending their title and later relegated by the Féderation Français de Football.

ONE COACH PER TOURNAMENT

Platini, the hero of 1984, was coach of the team which – in 1992 – became the first nation ever to win every match in its European qualifying group, but in Sweden, France were a disappointment, failing to qualify for the semi-finals. After the finals, Gérard Houllier took over the coaching reins.

Worse followed in 1993. After coasting through the first part of the qualifying competition, France needed just one point from two home games, against Israel and Bulgaria, to qualify for USA '94. In both games France took the lead and, with less than two minutes remaining, were 2–1 ahead of Israel and, a month later, drawing 1–1 with Bulgaria.

EURO FACT ***France were the second country to host the European Championship finals twice. The first time, in 1960, they finished fourth. The second time, in 1984, they won by beating Spain 2–0 in the Final.***

BLOSSOMING TALENT ***Sampdoria's young Christian Karembeu is part of France's new midfield***

Amazingly, both matches were lost. With the nation in a state of shock, Houllier resigned and Jacquet became France's third coach of the 1990s.

Platini, meanwhile, has his sights set on the 1998 World Cup finals. He is joint president of the French organizing committee.

FEAST FOLLOWS FAMINE

Jacquet must have wished he had a Platini in his team as the Euro96™ qualifying campaign got under way. France failed to score in their first three matches against Slovakia, Romania and Poland – all dangerous opponents. Fortunately, France also failed to concede any goals, either. A 2–0 win away to Azerbaijan broke the drought – which was then followed by another goalless draw, this time in Israel.

Speculation, inevitably, arose about whether Jacquet should lean towards the star system and try to mix together the explosive exiled talents of Jean-Pierre Papin (Bayern Munich), David Ginola (Newcastle United) and Eric Cantona (Manchester United).

In fact, Jacquet's own custom-made team spared him such considerations. France, in their last five matches, scored 20 goals including 10 at home to Azerbaijan. A campaign which had started so slowly ended with France joining Spain and Russia as the only undefeated nations.

SOLID FOUNDATIONS

Jacquet looks for a foundation towards the Paris Saint-Germain side who have brightened up the European club competitions throughout the 1990s. Players such as goalkeeper

Bernard Lama and centre back Alain Roche have been moulded into an effective partnerships with the likes of Monaco defender Eric Di Meco, Milan's versatile Desailly, Juventus playmaker Deschamps, as well as Sampdoria's Karembeu and his former Nantes team-mate Reynald Pedros.

The question is whether they can be effective enough to improve on the French showing at the last European finals. New star winger Zinedine Zidane, from Bordeaux, believes France can. He says: "We have the technical quality, we have the ambition. What we need now is to apply ourselves."

TOUGH DRAW

Coach Jacquet had made no secret of his desire to avoid Spain in the first round of the finals but that is precisely what the draw in Birmingham provided for the French, along with World Cup qualifying nemesis Bulgaria and the Romanians, whom France defeated impressively in Bucharest last October.

The three French goals that day came from Karembeu, Djorkaeff – voted top French player in the qualifying event – and Zidane, whose confidence developed almost overnight as Bordeaux surprised the rest of Europe as they took the UEFA Cup by storm in 1995–96.

Now he can bring that European veneer to bear at Newcastle and Leeds.

European Championship Record

1960	Fourth place
1964	Quarter-finalists
1968	Quarter-finalists
1972	did not qualify
1976	did not qualify
1980	did not qualify
1984	Winners
1988	did not qualify
1992	Group round

Aime Jacquet

Born on November 27, 1941. He played twice for France and completed a respected career as a midfielder with Saint-Etienne and Lyon before qualifying as a coach. He earned a reputation for turning out well-organized and disciplined teams during spells with Lyon, Bordeaux, Montpellier and Nancy before being appointed assistant to national coach Gérard Houllier. In December 1993 Jacquet succeeded Houllier following France's failure to qualify for the following year's World Cup finals.

NEW CHALLENGES AHEAD ***France's squad is ready to take on Europe in 1996 and the world in 1998***

"We should concentrate first and foremost on our own game before we start worrying about the opposition." *Zinedine Zidane, French midfielder.*

FRANCE

GERMANY

EURO96™ GROUP 7 WINNERS

GROUP C

No European nation has enjoyed as much national team success in the second half of the twentieth century as Germany. The statistics are awesome before one even takes account of the quality and class of the players involved.

The start mark was 1954 when West Germany won the World Cup for the first time with a shock victory over Hungary in Switzerland. The foundations for further success were laid in the early 1960s with the introduction of full-time professionalism and a unified championship instead of regional leagues.

STACKED WITH HONOURS

Since then, the Germans have failed to qualify for finals tournaments of the major events on only one occasion – that being the European Championship finals of 1968 (the Deutsches Fussball Bund (DFB) did not enter the first two competitions in 1960 and 1964). The honours piled up. European champions in 1972 and 1980, runners-up in 1976 and 1992; World Cup winners in 1974 and 1990, runners-up in 1966, 1982 and 1986 and third in 1970.

At club level, Bayern Munich won the European Champions' Cup three times in a row in the mid-1970s, also collecting the World Club Cup. Hamburg followed later as European champions. Borussia Dortmund, Bayern, Hamburg and Werder Bremen have all won the Cup Winners' Cup. Borussia Moenchengladbach (twice), Eintracht Frankfurt and Bayer Leverkusen have all triumphed in the UEFA Cup.

Such success also breeds pressure – as national coach Berti Vogts and his men found out following their defeats by Denmark in the European Championship Final of 1992 and by Bulgaria in the World Cup quarter-finals two years ago.

Critics called for wholesale changes, including the replacement of Vogts. But Vogts as a player was a terrier who never knew when he was beaten and, as a manager, he has proved much the same. He insisted after the traumatic defeats by both Denmark and Bulgaria that he would continue as the national coach as long as the DFB wanted him.

EURO FACT ***Both Germany's winning teams in 1972 and 1980 have featured a Müller – striker Gerd in 1972 and midfielder Hansi in 1980. Is that a pointer for Andreas Möller in 1996?***

OVERCOMING INJURIES

One of the traditional strengths of the German national team has been a comparative freedom from injury problems over the years. Until, that is, four years ago. Then injury robbed Germany of the services of their dynamic midfield leader Lotthar Matthäus for the European finals in Denmark just as injury denied them much-improved Matthias Sammer for the World Cup quarter-final against Bulgaria.

Matthäus, having suffered a recurrence of an old tendon injury, may not be playing at Euro96™, the captaincy armband having been handed on to a player with immense knowledge of the challenges of playing competitive football around Europe – striker Jürgen Klinsmann, of Bayern Munich, a veteran of the Italian, French and English leagues.

SHOULDER TO SHOULDER ***Newcomer Christian Ziege is an accomplished left-side defender***

"As long as I am enjoying the job."

BERTI VOGTS, *German coach, on being asked how long he would stay in charge.*

HARDY PERENNIALS ***Germany are always a force to be reckoned with in the major tournaments***

Sammer, however, does expect to be present to demonstrate just how significant a figure he has become in European football. Sammer, son of a former East German international, was switched back to sweeper/playmaker on his return to German football after a depressing six months in Italy with one of Klinsmann's old clubs, Internazionale. German fans expect him to guide the national team now just as he guided Dortmund to the 1995 league title.

TALENT IN ALL POSITIONS

Around him will be the expected plethora of talent. Ollie Kahn and Andy Kopke are highly competitive rivals for the goalkeeping jersey; Christian Ziege is one of the finest young left defenders in Europe; Thomas Hässler is always trying the unpredictable angles in midfield; and Klinsmann has a fiery new partner up front in Heiko Herrlich.

Germany's approach to tournaments is invariably the same: a slow start with vital results achieved right on cue. Their qualifying campaign followed that pattern. The Germans' first five games included a pair of struggling wins by 2–1 against Albania and a 1–1 home draw against Wales. But, in the space of four days in October 1995, Moldova were beaten 6–1 in Germany, Wales by 2–1 in Cardiff.

Suddenly, Germany were cruising. Just what their fans expect of Berti Vogts and his men in the finals.

European Championship Record

	WEST GERMANY	EAST GERMANY
1960	did not enter	First Round
1964	did not enter	Second Round
1968	did not qualify	did not qualify
1972	Champions	did not qualify
1976	Runners-up	did not qualify
1980	Champions	did not qualify
1984	Group Round	did not qualify
1988	Semi-final	did not qualify
1992	Runners-up (competed as united Germany)	

Berti Vogts

Born December 30, 1946. Vogts's appointment in 1990, succeeding Franz Beckenbauer after the World Cup win in Rome, maintained the tradition that every manager of Germany since World War II has been an international. Vogts joined Borussia Moenchengladbach in 1965. Two years later, he made the first of 96 senior appearances in defence for West Germany. Vogts played 419 league games for Borussia, won the World Cup in 1974, two UEFA Cups, five Bundesliga titles and German Cup once. He played in the team which lost on penalties to Czechoslovakia in the 1976 European final. Vogts was twice voted footballer of the year in Germany and joined the German federation coaching staff in 1979.

Czech Republic

HALLMARK OF QUALITY

EURO96™ GROUP 5 WINNERS

GROUP C

The Czech Republic are competing at the finals of an international championship for the first time – in this guise. Yet, whatever changes have been wrought by the political developments of the twentieth century, the history of Czech football remains a guarantee of quality for any team bearing that name.

Football in the region first centred on the Bohemia of the years before World War One. Then came the newly-integrated state of Czechoslovakia. Eventually, at the start of the 1990s, the Czechs and the Slovaks decided to go their separate ways – and the national football association had to split at the conclusion of the 1994 World Cup qualifying competition.

BOHEMIAN RHAPSODIES

As in the early days, so now, the great rivals of Prague club football – Sparta and Slavia – provide the backbone of the national squad, guided by coach Dusan Uhrin.

Czechoslovakia's record in major competitions is the best of all the old Eastern Bloc nations. They reached the World Cup Final in both 1934 and 1962 – as well as making six other appearances in the finals – and were European Champions in 1976.

At club level, too, Czech clubs were among the cream of Europe. In 1927, Sparta Prague were the first winners of the Mitropa Cup – the fore-runner of the modern UEFA competitions.

EURO FACT ***Czechoslovakia won the 1976 European title by defeating West Germany 5–3 in a penalty shoot-out after a 2–2 draw in the Final in Belgrade. Four years later, in Italy, they beat their hosts in another shoot-out after a goalless draw in the Third Place Play-off in Naples. The score, this time, was 9–8.***

CZECHS BOUNCE BACK

The present European Championship is the first event in which the Czech Republic have competed as such. Most critics expected the qualifying effort to prove too much for a team shorn of a Slovak contribution.

Such scepticism appeared justified when, after a good start, the Czechs lost 1–0 away to the minnows of Luxembourg, arguably the biggest shock of the qualifying competition. That was the result which, it appeared, would offer Norway and Holland the opportunity to take command of the group.

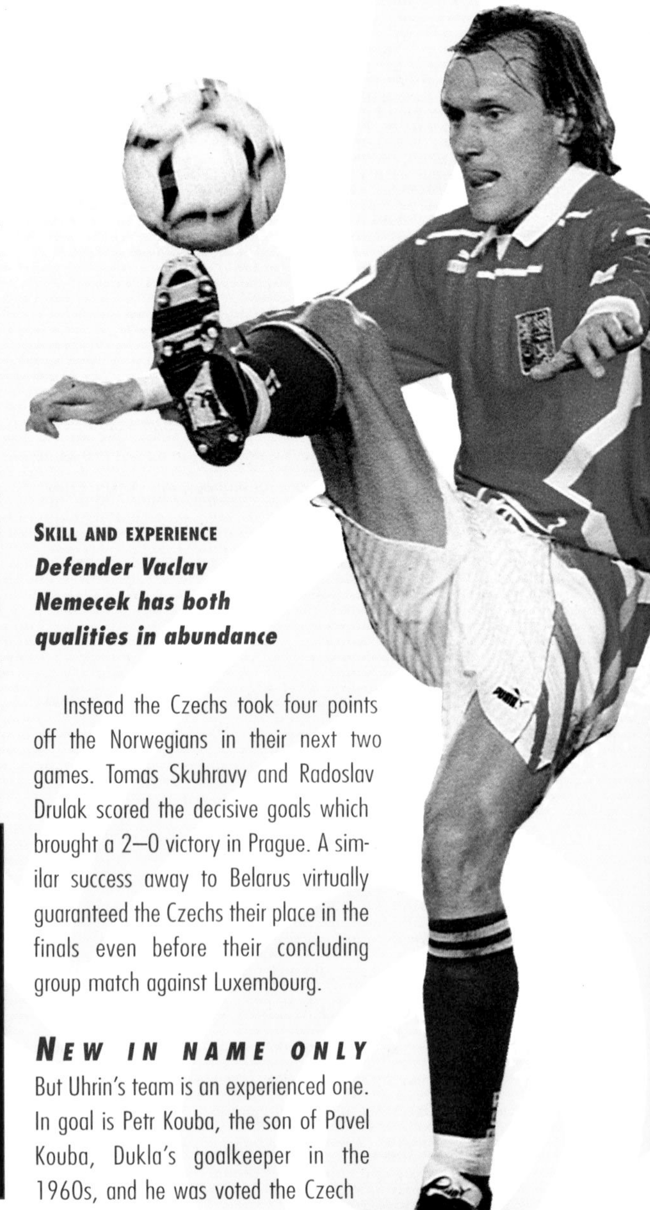

SKILL AND EXPERIENCE
Defender Vaclav Nemecek has both qualities in abundance

Instead the Czechs took four points off the Norwegians in their next two games. Tomas Skuhravy and Radoslav Drulak scored the decisive goals which brought a 2–0 victory in Prague. A similar success away to Belarus virtually guaranteed the Czechs their place in the finals even before their concluding group match against Luxembourg.

NEW IN NAME ONLY

But Uhrin's team is an experienced one. In goal is Petr Kouba, the son of Pavel Kouba, Dukla's goalkeeper in the 1960s, and he was voted the Czech

New names, new faces ***The Czech Republic's team will have a great tradition to uphold***

"I am sure we can do well in the finals because we have such a well-balanced mixture of youth and experience." Patrik Berger, Czech midfielder.

Republic's top player of the qualifying competition by an international jury of media experts assembled by one of the major event sponsors.

In front of Kouba, the Czechs benefit from the full weight of experience developed from the former Czechoslovakia. Solidly-built sweeper Miroslav Kadlec and tall and powerful Vaclav Nemecek at stopper are both veterans of the 1990 World Cup campaign, when Czechoslovakia reached the quarter-finals in Italy, before losing to the Germans – against whom they will now seek revenge at Old Trafford, Manchester, on June 9.

Ironically, it is the transfer-hunting German clubs which have both upset and helped to develop the Czech midfield. Manager Uhrin had to rebuild his creative unit in the wake of a string of departures for the Bundesliga, but that did provide the opportunity for the vastly talented Patrik Berger to establish himself in the team who completed their qualifying programme in style.

By then Berger himself had been snapped up by Borussia Dortmund but the player has no doubt about the manner in which he and his country will profit. Berger says: "We do not underestimate opposition such as Italy, Germany and Russia."

Berger will no doubt draw on the experience he gained with Dortmund in the 1995–96 UEFA Champions League when it comes to representing his country at European international level. His partnerships with Pavel Kuka, with Skuhravy and with the new hero, Drulak from little-known Drnovice, promise trouble ahead for even the world-class defences in their way at Euro96™.

This Czech Republic team represent the best of the old and the new.

European Championship Record

Competed as Czechoslovakia until 1992

1960	Third place
1964	First round
1968	did not qualify
1972	did not qualify
1976	Winners
1980	Third place
1984	did not qualify
1988	did not qualify
1992	did not qualify

Dusan Uhrin

Born on February 5, 1943. He was appointed national team manager of the newly-independent Czech Republic in 1993 after impressive work with record champions Sparta of Prague. Initially he made his name as a youth coach at Sparta and in two spells with Rude Hvezda of Cheb. He coached Bohemians Prague and the Czechoslovak under-21 side before returning to Sparta in 1991.

ITALY

EURO96™ GROUP 4 RUNNERS-UP

GROUP C

Italy, for all their star-studded reputation, are perhaps the greatest under-achievers of recent European international football. For most of the last 20 years, the Italian league has produced the highest average attendances in Europe. Italian clubs have spent larger sums in harvesting more international superstars and won more trophies than any other championship.

Yet, for all the money and all the passion, Italy have won the World Cup only once in the last 50 years and have only once won the European Championship – and that was only after a replay in their own backyard.

GALAXY OF STARS

The likes of Gianni Rivera, Sandro Mazzola, Luigi Riva, Giacinto Facchetti, Dino Zoff and Roberto Baggio have long since earned permanent places in football's international hall of fame. Yet successive Italian national managers have struggled – often in vain – to construct teams in which such great players could freely express their talent.

Most countries would hail as inspired the manager who achieved a World Cup silver medal. But not Italy. Arrigo Sacchi returned from the World Cup Final defeat on penalties at the hands of Brazil and entered the Euro96™ qualifying competition amid continuing discussion over the contrasting merits of his tactical approach compared with that of fellow coaches such as Giovanni Trapattoni (Cagliari), Zdenek Zeman (Lazio) and Marcello Lippi (Juventus).

EURO FACT ***Italy used four goalkeepers in their 10 qualifying matches – Gianluca Pagliuca, Angelo Peruzzi, Lucca Bucci and Francesco Toldo. Fiorentina's Toldo appeared as substitute in the 1-1 draw against Croatia in Split after Bucci was sent off in the ninth minute. The outfield player withdrawn was Gianfranco Zola.***

WINNING STYLE ***Fabrizio Ravanelli shoots for goal during Italy's 3-1 victory over Ukraine***

At least Sacchi has succeeded where his predecessor Angelo Vicini failed last time out, in taking Italy to the European finals. Not that it was easy.

The draw, which placed Italy in a group otherwise populated by eastern European newcomers, proved deceptive. Despite the success achieved in *Calcio* of players such as Zvonimir Boban and Alen Boksic, the Italian game was unprepared for the brazen confidence with which Croatia attacked – and beat – them in Palermo. Only three matches into the qualifying competition and Italy were misfiring badly.

WORLD CUP HANGOVER

One reason why they took so long to get into their stride was the fatigue induced by the 1994 World Cup campaign. Sacchi's successor as coach at Milan, Fabio Capello, admitted freely that even such great players as Paolo Maldini spent the first half of the 1994–95 season recovering from a physical and psychological Pasadena hangover.

Sacchi was not helped by the post-World Cup injuries which plagued Roberto Baggio, the retirement of sweeper Franco Baresi and the need to find a new goalkeeper. On top of that, Gianluca Vialli, after two injury-plagued seasons, emerged as a decisive force in Juventus' 1995 league title-winning side – without showing any inclination to play for his country.

But every cloud has a silver lining. In Italy's case, there were two. One was the brilliant form of Parma's goalscoring playmaker, Gianfranco Zola – their leading scorer in the qualifying campaign with seven goals, including a hat-trick in the concluding 4–0 victory over Lithuania. The other was the explosion of Juventus wonderboy Alessandro Del Piero.

SURFEIT OF SUPER TALENT

In the 1995–96 UEFA Champions League, Del Piero managed a goal in each of Juve's first five games. He is, without any doubt, the new golden boy. The challenge for Sacchi is to fit him into the Italian national team with more consistent success than so many superstar predecessors.

The identity of his partner up front may remain in doubt right up until the start of the finals. Sacchi admires both Juventus' Fabrizio Ravanelli and Lazio's Pierluigi Casiraghi, but the need to balance his team means they are unlikely – barring injuries – to play side by side.

At the end of 1995, Sacchi's managerial record with the *Azzurri* was just six defeats in 44 games. But he was quick to warn Italy's players and supporters against discounting the threat posed by Russia and the Czech Republic, saying: "It would be dangerous for us to put too much attention on our game against Germany. We have made mistakes in the past by under-estimating opponents."

European Championship Record

1960	did not enter
1964	Second round
1968	Winners
1972	Quarter-finalists
1976	did not qualify
1980	Fourth place
1984	did not qualify
1988	Semi-finalists
1992	did not qualify

Arrigo Sacchi

Born on April 1, 1946. He succeeded Angelo Vicini in the autumn of 1991 after a hugely-successful five years in which he led Milan to two European Champion Clubs' Cups, two league titles and two World Club Championships. Sacchi was never a top league player and began his coaching career with Cesena youth team in 1977. He qualified from the Coverciano coaching centre that same year and was appointed to his first senior post – with third division Rimini – in 1982. In 1985, he took over Parma, bringing them out of Serie C, before succeeding Nils Liedholm at Milan in 1987.

NO ILLUSIONS ***Italy look determined before their qualifier against Ukraine in Bari in November***

"If we want to do well at Euro96™ we dare not make the mistake of underestimating opponents again." *Arrigo Sacchi, Italian coach.*

ITALY

RUSSIA

EURO96™ GROUP 8 WINNERS

RUSSIAN BEAR SHEDS ITS COAT

GROUP C

With one Championship victory and three defeats in the Final, the Soviet Union were the most consistent team in the history of the European Championship. Now it is up to Russia, the republic which was the main supplier of players to the great Soviet teams, to carry the flag in the modern era.

Russian football will be represented in yet a third different guise at Euro96™. Five times the republic provided the majority of the members of the national squad of the Soviet Union – in 1960, 1964, 1968, 1972 and 1988. Then, four years ago, the collapse of the Soviet Union meant it was under the banner of the Commonwealth of Independent States (CIS), along with team-mates from Ukraine, Belarus and Georgia, that they competed in Sweden. But, appearances can be deceptive. Any opponents who believe that the power and strength inherent in the Russian is no longer leavened by the imagination and technical skills from the southern republics would be seriously mistaken.

When the CIS went the way of the Soviet Union, the former Soviet international footballers were offered a one-off option: to play for their own new republics or to continue their international careers with the new Russia. Most, recognizing that the new republics would need time to build, opted to stay with Russia. Ukrainians such as striker Sergei Yuran and right-winger Andrei Kanchelskis will thus carry the Russian threat to the rest of Europe.

EURO FACT ***Lev Yashin, greatest Russian footballer and perhaps the best goalkeeper of all time, was the Soviet Union's keeper when they beat Yugoslavia 2–1 in the first final in the old Parc des Princes in Paris in 1960. Yashin, originally an ice hockey goalkeeper, won 78 caps between 1954 and 1967. He was 1963 European Footballer of the Year.***

FOUR-TIME FINALISTS

It is a dangerous mixture, as the Soviet record in the European Championship proves. They were winners of the inaugural event in 1960, runners-up on three occasions – to Spain in 1964, to West Germany in 1972 and to Holland in 1988 – and finished fourth in 1968.

Appropriately, it was Russia who emerged as the first of the qualifiers to join hosts England in the finals when they beat Greece, 2–1 in Moscow, in mid-October 1995 (Spain qualified on the same day, but only later in the evening). Such an early marker will help provide the confidence so sadly lacking at the World Cup in 1994, when a player power revolt and other personality clashes wrecked any chance they had of challenging Brazil and Sweden for first-round group domination.

BACK TO FRONT ***Vassili Koulkov brings the ball out of defence against Finland***

Twists and turns ***Andre Kanchelskis torments a Finnish defender during Russia's 6–0 away win***

Black Sheep Back in Fold

Russia turned the international corner after the 1994 World Cup finals. Coach Pavel Sadyrin was replaced, and Moscow Spartak manager Oleg Romantsev was handed additional, simultaneous responsibility for the national team. He immediately sought to recall many of Sadyrin's "black sheep". One of the last to earn a recall was Yuran, who missed the World Cup but returned to Spartak after spells in Portugal with Benfica.

The qualifying round success demonstrated perfectly, as national team aide Leonid Trakhtenberg said, how "in a short time, Romantsev has managed to create real teamwork and also melt the ice of hostility between the players."

Russia opened their qualifying programme in decisive style in October, 1994, defeating San Marino 4–0 in Moscow. An important 1–1 draw, away to Scotland in Glasgow, came next, but it was not until experienced forward Igor Dobrovolski returned to national team duty in the spring of 1995 that the attack began to function smoothly.

Greek Tragedies

A 3–0 victory away to fellow 1994 World Cup finalists Greece not only punctured Greek aspirations but also secured Russian confidence. After this came a 7–0 rout of San Marino in Serravalle and a 6–0 defeat Finland in Helsinki – followed by the all-important return victory over Greece in Moscow.

Goals from Yuri Kovtun and captain Viktor Onopko brought Russia this second victory over Greece, which maintained their unbeaten record in Group 8 with one match to play. Trakhtenberg said: "It was a key game." Finland were duly beaten in Moscow to confirm Russia's status as group winners.

Critics used to claim that the problem of Russian football was a failure to turn disciplined approach play into goals. The rest of Europe should be warned: Romantsev's new Russia appear to have found the answer.

European Championship Record

1960	Champions (USSR)
1964	Runners-up (USSR)
1968	Fourth place (USSR – lost semi-final coin toss)
1972	Runners-up (USSR)
1976	Quarter-finalists (USSR)
1980	did not qualify (USSR)
1984	did not qualify (USSR)
1988	Runners-up (USSR)
1992	Group round (CIS)

Oleg Romantsev

Born January 4, 1954. Romantsev is a former Soviet international left-back who played 10 times for the USSR, scoring one goal. He was a star pupil of veteran coach Konstantin Beskov, for many years boss of both Moscow Spartak and the Soviet national team. Romantsev, who began playing with Automobilist of Krasnoyarsk, was Spartak's left-back in the late 1970s and a member of the Soviet bronze medal team at the 1980 Moscow Olympic Games. A qualified physical education graduate, he became Beskov's aide after retiring, then coached third division Krasnaya Presniya and Orzhonkidze Spartak before returning to Spartak as first-team coach in 1989. National team duties were added in the summer of 1994 after Russia's disappointing World Cup campaign.

"We needed to finish first, not second. We wanted the team not only to go to England but to go as one of the favourites."

Leonid Trakhtenberg, national team aide, after the defeat of Greece in October 1995.

DENMARK

EURO96™ GROUP 2 RUNNERS-UP

GROUP D

Denmark's victory in the European Championship finals in Sweden two years ago was a football miracle.

Denmark had not even qualified for the finals and were called up only at the last moment – in controversial circumstances – to replace Yugoslavia, who were frozen out when the governing bodies of international football decided to interpret United Nations sanctions as raising a sporting as well as a diplomatic barrier.

The Danes pulled their squad back together at the last moment and, after a slow start, defeated Holland on penalties in the semi-finals then Germany by 2–0 in the Final in Gothenburg with goals from midfielders John Jensen and Kim Vilfort.

INTO THE LIMELIGHT

Denmark counted among Europe's minnows until, in 1971, steps were taken towards ending the grip of amateurism on the domestic game. Less than a decade later open professional was cleared and two years ago the emerging Brondby club became the first to go full-time professional. Much of the impetus came from a former exiled professional named Finn Laudrup, an international in his day, but whose fame has long since been eclipsed by that of his sons Michael and Brian.

Such domestic progress was not reflected internationally until the 1984 European Championship came around. By that time the Danes had discovered two players of world-class talent whose example inspired a generation: Allan Simonsen and Morten Olsen. They qualified for the finals in France ahead of England, but Simonsen lucklessly broke his leg in the opening game. However, with a commanding figure such as Olsen at the back, Denmark roared on to the semi-finals and a shoot-out defeat by Spain.

EURO FACT ***Kim Vilfort, one of Denmark's heroes in 1992, flew home from Sweden in the middle of the finals after his daughter was taken ill. When her condition improved his wife persuaded him to rejoin his team-mates – which he did, in time to score Denmark's decisive second goal in the Final victory over Germany.***

ON TARGET ***Denmark's Mikkel Beck (red shirt) nets the second goal in their 3–1 win over Armenia***

DEFENDING CHAMPIONS ***Denmark will not have the element of surprise this time***

European Championship Record

1960	First round
1964	Fourth place
1968	did not qualify
1972	did not qualify
1976	did not qualify
1980	did not qualify
1984	Semi-finalists
1988	Group round
1992	Winners

Richard Moller Nielsen

Born on August 19, 1937 and will end his managerial term with Denmark when his contract expires at the finals' end. He was twice an international player for Denmark, performing in the centre of defence with a determination which earned the nickname of "Lionheart." Injury ended his playing career prematurely, but he was an immediate success as a coach. With Odense he won the league title in 1977 and 1982 and coached the national Olympic and under-21 teams. Moller Nielsen was an assistant to Sepp Piontek whom he succeeded as national coach in 1990.

ROCKY ROAD TO ENGLAND

The Danes began their title defence inauspiciously. A draw away to Macedona, a home win over Belgium, a 3–0 defeat un Spain and a 1–1 draw in Cyprus was hardly the stuff of champions. The key to qualification fell in September 1995 when Denmark travelled to Brussels to face Belgium. Spain were clearly going to win the group. The contest was between Danes and Belgians for second place.

Belgium, as hosts, were narrow favourites. But Denmark produced a display worthy of their champions' crown to win 3–1 with goals from Michael Laudrup, Mikkel Beck and Vilfort. A "safe" 1–1 draw at home to Spain was followed by a comfortable 3–1 home win over Armenia. Denmark were group runners-up – six points clear of Belgium.

A NEW LOOK

The Danes have changed significantly since winning the European title four years ago in Gothenburg. Gone is the veteran sweeper and skipper Lars Olsen, Jensen was relegated to the midfield fringes and striker Fleming Povlsen retired.

At least Michael Laudrup, possibly Denmark's greatest ever player, has made his peace with manager Moller Nielsen and been welcomed back into the squad. He has maintained his international high profile with his championship inspiring performances in Spain for first Barcelona, then Real Madrid.

Peter Schmeichel remains one of the world's most redoubtable goalkeepers and a great character – as his burst upfield to score a late goal for Manchester United in their UEFA Cup tie against Rotor Volgograd last September demonstrated. The defence has rapidly developed its understanding, with two home players – Silkeborg's John Laursen and Jens Risager of Brondby – and West Ham United's Marc Rieper and Fenerbahce's Jes Hogh, who have both improved immensely thanks to their experiences playing abroad.

In midfield, Vilfort can hold his position with great tactical awareness, tackle cleanly and burst forward through a channel on the right when the opposition least expected, though, at 33, he will be one of the oldest players at the finals. Denmark are fortunate to have discovered younger players such as Allan Nielsen and Morten Wieghorst, both 25, who are able to both win the ball and use it widely in areas where the Laudrup brothers can wreak the most damage.

"We may not win the European title again. But you can be assured we will not make it easy for anyone who wants to take the title from us." *Michael Laudrup, Danish star.*

PORTUGAL

EBULLIENCE AND CHARM

EURO 96™ GROUP 6 WINNERS

GROUP D

Portugal are among the most interesting – as well as being among the best – national teams in Europe. They were extremely unlucky to miss out on the 1994 World Cup finals, falling just short in the qualifying group which was headed by Switzerland and the eventual runners-up Italy.

That summed up, for many years, the status of Portugal as the "nearly men" of European international football – a label they are still trying to lose some 130 years after the game was first brought to the country by British university students and visiting sailors.

Three clubs have dominated the domestic scene: Benfica and Sporting of Lisbon and Porto, have won the Portuguese championship every season for the last 50 years – Belenenses were champions in 1946.

Portugal's most successful World Cup campaign was in England, in 1966 when, led by the brilliant Eusebio, they finished third. Their finest European Championship was 1984 in France. Once again the semi-final was as far as they went, the hosts beating them 3–2 in a classic encounter.

RELIANCE ON YOUTH

In the late 1980s, the federation engaged a former goalkeeper, Carlos Queiroz, to reorganize the game at youth national level and he produced a brilliant teenage side which twice won the World Youth Cup. This, in turn, reawakened interest and concern for the senior national team.

Queiroz resigned after the 1994 World Cup qualifying failure, but his work has been carried on successfully by former assistant Antonio Oliveira.

It may not be coincidental that Portugal's national team renaissance coincides with the profitable player-export era in their history. Few Portuguese players had tried their luck abroad in earlier years. Occasionally one would cross the borders into Spanish or French football briefly but little more, and with little success.

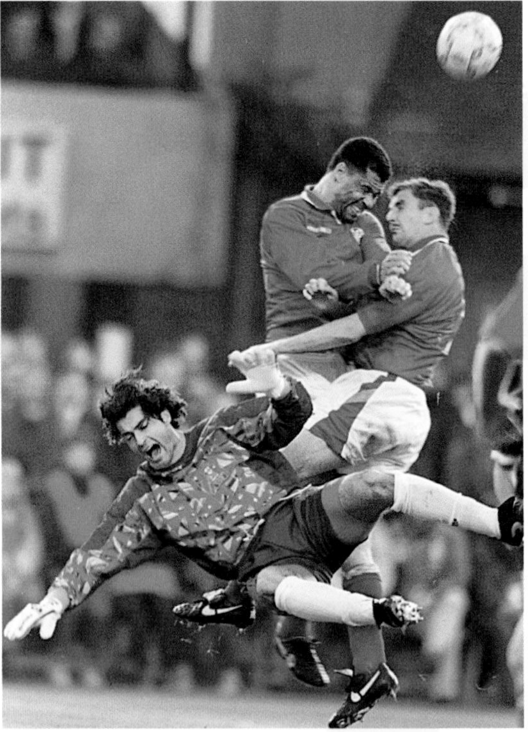

NO WAY ***Vitor Baia repels an Irish Republic raid***

LIRA LURE FOR LISBON LADS

The success of Portugal's youth team, however, drew admiring spies from all around Europe – especially from Italy. Thus forward Rui Barros, then midfielder Paulo Sousa joined Juventus, Rui Costa went to Fiorentina and Fernando Couto joined Parma. As for the magically-gifted but injury-battered Paulo Futre, he joined Spain's Atletico Madrid then Italy's Reggiana and Milan.

Portugal set out their Euro96™ stall the way they meant to continue, with a 2–1 victory over Northern Ireland in Belfast. They lost only once – going down 1–0 to the Irish Republic in Dublin when goalkeeper – and captain – Vitor Baia allowed a cross-shot from Steve Staunton to skid through his fingers for the only goal.

Portugal had their revenge. On the last matchday, the Irish came back to Lisbon and, despite the support of 20,000 travelling fans, were soundly thrashed 3–0. Rui Costa, Helder Cristovao and Jorge Cadete scored the goals which sent Portugal into the finals as group winners and with the aura of dangerous outsiders.

EURO FACT ***Nine of the Portugal's Euro96™ hopefuls featured in their 1991 World Youth Cup-winning squad – Figo, Peixe, Rui Costa, Jorge Costa, Abel Xavier, Nelson, Rui Bento, Joao Vieira Pinto and Tulipa.***

"Our young players are our strength. We've placed our faith in them and they have never let us down." *Antonio Oliveira, Portugal's coach, on his team's youthfulness.*

PORTUGAL

CHRISTMAS COMES EARLY

Events at Wembley and Birmingham in the fortnight before Christmas left the Portuguese feeling confident about their prospects.

First they secured a well-deserved 1–1 draw with Euro96™ hosts England in a friendly, thanks to a second-half strike from substitute Paulo Alves. Portugal's 4–3–2–1 formation, with Paulo Sousa orchestrating many of their best moves from midfield, earned widespread praise. Although the match at Wembley was a friendly, Portugal demonstrated fluidity in attack and were quick to defend in depth. England coach Terry Venables described them afterwards as: "One of the best teams, with Brazil, we have played."

Then, five days later, the draw for the finals placed them in possibly the least daunting of the groups alongside Denmark, Croatia and Turkey.

Significantly, the Wembley squad included, in Dani Carvalho and Nuno Gomes, two further highly-promising products of their youth system. Either player – or even both – could force their way into Portugal's line-up by the time they open their English campaign for real against Denmark at Hillsborough, Sheffield, on June 9.

Portugal's finest performance in the World Cup came in England. Can history repeat itself, 30 years later, on the European stage?

European Championship Record

1960	Quarter-finalists
1964	First round
1968	did not qualify
1972	did not qualify
1976	did not qualify
1980	did not qualify
1984	Semi-finalists
1988	did not qualify
1992	did not qualify

Antonio Oliveira

Born on June 10, 1952. He was originally a midfielder with FC Porto, Penafiel and Sporting for whom he scored 107 goals in 228 league games. Oliveira also played for Real Betis of Seville (Spain) before launching his senior coaching career with Nacional of Madeira in 1985. Later he took charge of Vitoria Guimaraes, Academica Coimbra, Gil Vicente and Sporting Braga before being appointed technical director of the national team set-up in December, 1994.

DANGEROUS OUTSIDERS ***Portugal boast some of the finest young talent in Europe***

TURKEY

EURO96™ GROUP 3 WINNERS

GROUP D

MIDFIELD MAESTRO ***Oguz Cetin leads the Turkish invasion force from midfield***

Turkey have never reached the finals of the European Championship before. Indeed, they have appeared only once in their history at the finals of a major event and that was the World Cup back in 1954. On that occasion they needed a blind boy, pulling out lots after a drawn play-off against Spain, to earn their place in the finals.

This time nothing was left to such accidents. Turkey opened their qualifying campaign with a 2–2 draw away to Hungary in Budapest then thrashed Iceland 5–0. The result which made Europe sit up and take Turkey seriously, however, was a 2–1 win away to Switzerland in Bern in April last year. Goals from Hakan Sukur – known familarly by his first name only – his fourth in five games, and Ogun lifted Turkey to the top of the group. After that they were rarely in danger – to the gun-firing delight of their excitable supporters.

FANATICAL SUPPORT

Turkey's fans are renowned as among the most passionate in Europe and they will provide enormous encouragement for their players in the European finals. As Brad Friedel, imported American goalkeeper of top club Galatasaray, says: "The media and the fans keep you under pressure all the time. But we all accept that, as professional footballers, we get paid very well for being a footballer so that's the price on the ticket."

More than 40 foreign players now operate in the Turkish championship, mainly from Europe and Africa. They have helped to raise standards at domestic level – Scottish coach Graeme Souness, who took over last summer at Galatasaray, says: "Football is still developing here and there are things they are keen to learn from the rest of Europe. Turkey have players who could, if they were mentally strong enough, play successfully anywhere in the world."

EURO FACT ***National coach Fatih Terim made his playing debut for Turkey in the European Championship – in a 1–1 draw against Switzerland in April 1975 in the 1976 event's qualifying competition.***

HOME IS WHERE THE HEART IS

One of the few Turkish players who tried the foreign experience and did not enjoy it was tall striker Hakan. His exploits in the European Championship qualifying competition earned a transfer last summer to the Italian club, Torino. Within three months, however, and despite some promising performances, he grew homesick. Galatasaray paid a reported £3 million to take him home and rebuild his confidence to serve the national cause at Euro96™.

Attacking partners are likely to include Trabzonspor's Hami Mandirali and one of the emerging new heroes of Turkish football in Ertugrul Saglam.

Behind him, Turkey's midfield inspiration depends on veteran Oguz Cetin from another of the country's great Istanbul clubs, Fenerbahce. Oguz, at 33, is the oldest outfield player in the Turkish squad. Along the qualifying path, he overtook the Turkish record of 51 international appearances which had been set by Fatih Terim, who is now his national team manager.

The third of the big Istanbul clubs are Besiktas who provide three of Turkey's defensive stalwarts in Alpay Ozalan, Recep Cetin and Gokhan Keskin with more than 100 international appearances between them.

Seeing the excitement football generates now in Turkey, it is hard to believe that the game was outlawed in the early years of this century after being introduced in 1899 at the Galatasaray High School in Istanbul. Public pressure was such, however, that a league championship was initiated in 1905, though it was not until 1923 that the national team marked their debut with a 2–2 draw at home to Romania.

FOREIGN INFLUENCE

However, a full national championship was not launched until 1960, when foreign players and coaches began – better late than never compared with most of the rest of Europe – to help make up for lost time. Among these coaches was George Dick, a Scottish inside forward, who was followed with varying degrees of success by fellow Britons such as Brian Birch, Don Howe, Malcolm Allison and – most successful of all – Gordon Milne at Besiktas.

Later the emphasis shifted towards German expertise with Jupp Derwall and Sepp Piontek among the big-name imports. Among Derwall's pupils was the man who has just led Turkey to their greatest achievement thus far, Fatih Terim.

European Championship Record

1960	First round
1964	First round
1968	did not qualify
1972	did not qualify
1976	did not qualify
1980	did not qualify
1984	did not qualify
1988	did not qualify
1992	did not qualify

Fatih Terim

Born in Adana on September 14, 1953, Fatih Terim was for many years holder of the Turkish international appearances record with 51 caps. A central defender, then sweeper, he made his name with Adanademirspor and then spent 13 years with Galatasaray. After retiring, he coached Ankaragucu and Goztepe Izmir and was appointed national under-21 coach in 1990. He became assistant to national coach Sepp Piontek whom he duly succeeded in July 1993.

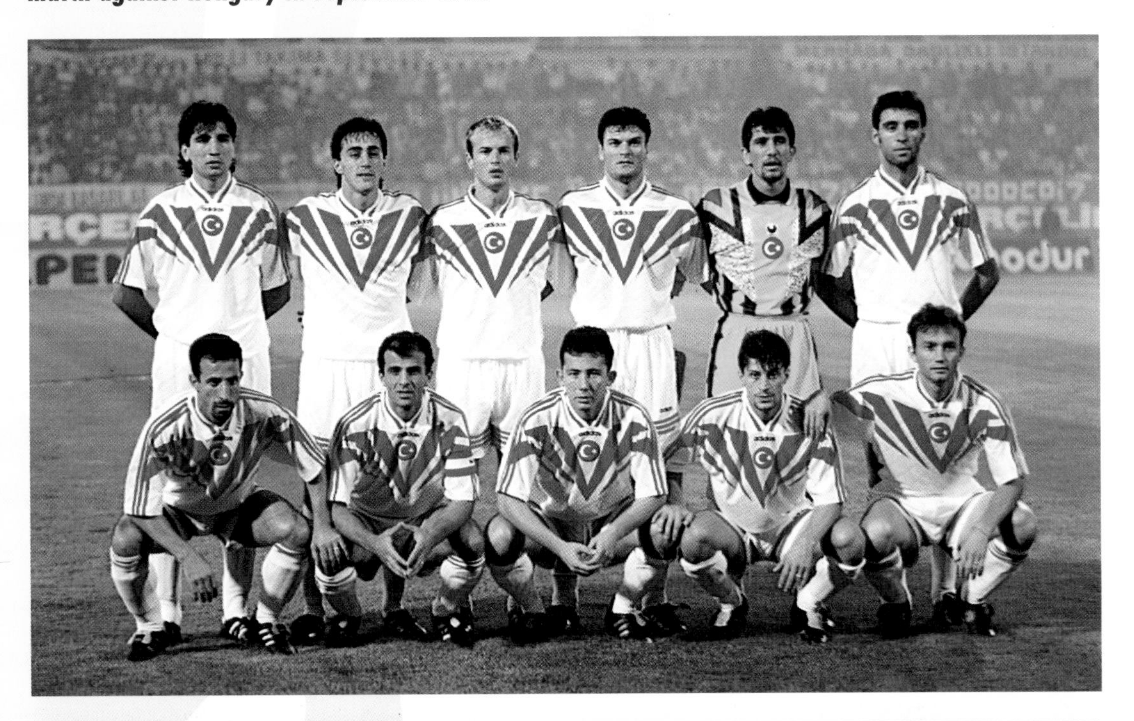

INTO BATTLE ***Turkey line up before their qualifying match against Hungary in September 1995***

"Turkey have some very talented players. You can't deny the pace at which they're making progress." *Graeme Souness, Galatasaray coach.*

CROATIA

EURO96™ GROUP 4 WINNERS

GROUP D

Croatia was one of the largest states which formed the Balkan nation of Yugoslavia. In the aftermath of Marshall Tito's death, the states reverted to their earlier independence and Croatia has worked hard to get to the very top of the European tree, a position almost enjoyed by Yugoslavia in two previous European Championships.

As the draw for the qualifying tournament for Euro96™ was progressing at the television studios in Manchester, Italian smiles were growing ever broader. It produced not one but five new eastern European nations as opponents for Italy on the road to England.

Apart from Ukraine – built around the proven international talents of Kiev Dynamo – there was no known force to upset the Azzurri on the majestic progress which their status as world No. 2 deserved. However, Italy discovered – as the rest of the best of Europe may come to realize in England – that Croatia are underrated at their opponents' peril.

ITALIANS SHOCKED

The point was forcibly brought home to Europe's international soccer-watchers on November 16, 1994, in the Stadio La Favorita in Palermo. Croatia had provided a handful of outstanding individuals to Italy's Serie A in full-back Robert Jarni, midfielder Zvonimir Boban at Milan and centre-forward Alen Boksic at Lazio.

But they had much more to offer as Italian coach Arrigo Sacchi and superstars Paolo Maldini and Roberto Baggio discovered. That "extra" included goalkeeper Drazen Ladic, midfield playmaker Robert Prosinecki (then with Oviedo in Spain, now with Barcelona) and the Sevilla striker Davor Suker.

It was Suker who scored the decisive goals in the 32nd and 60th minutes. Dino Baggio pulled one back for Italy in second half injury-time but it was too little much too late. Croatia, born of the bloody collapse of the former Yugoslavia, had achieved their most remarkable international football result in their brief history.

EURO FACT ***Croatia's reconstituted national federation was founded in 1991 – and admitted to FIFA a year later. But that was just too late for Croatia to enter the 1994 World Cup qualifiers.***

CHECKED ***Luigi Apolloni of Italy tries to contain Croats Zvonimir Boban (10) and Alen Boksic (11)***

ABSENT FRIENDS

The majority of Croatia's players are based with clubs abroad. But that has done nothing to dissipate their national pride. As Suker says: "The very fact of everything our country has gone through in the last couple of years makes us all the more determined to do well. Our people at home have had little enough to cheer them in the last few years. We want to give them something – even if it is 'just' football – of which they can be proud. National pride is worth at least one goal to us."

Croatia are not, in fact, total newcomers to international football. The country existed as an independent political – and thus football – entity, albeit under puppet regime conditions, in the 1940s. The Croats organized their own league championship and their own national team. But, under direction from Berlin, they played against only other Axis-aligned nations such as Germany, Italy, Bulgaria and Romania.

Croatia remained a significant source of football strength and talent within the former Yugoslavia after the war. Dinamo Zagreb and Hajduk Split built impressive records in European club competitions – which they have extended since Croatia's independent re-emergence in 1990.

The first match of the new era was a 2–0 win over Romania in Rijeka on December 22, 1990. Zlatko Kranjcar scored the historic opening goal and Ladic, Jarni and Boban are expected to be the "survivors" from that match who lead out Croatia in June for their first-ever appearance in the finals of a major tournament.

SUKER PUNCHES

Croatia opened their qualifying account with a 2–0 win over Estonia in Tallinn on September 4, 1994. Suker scored both goals, as he did against Italy and then again in a surprisingly decisive 4–0 win over a Ukraine side who proved to be the major disappointment of the group. Ukraine found a vestige of form at last in June last year, defeating Croatia 1–0 in Kiev. But it was not enough to disturb Croatia's three-point lead over Italy at the top of the table.

Nor could Croatian confidence be upset by Italy's loudly-stated reluctance to play the return match in their qualifying group in their country. The Italians were persuaded, in the end, to play in Split, where a 1–1 draw cleared Croatia's path to the finals more effectively than Italy's, and it meant that victory in Slovenia in the final qualifier would guarantee a first-place finish in the group, irrespective of the Italians' results. Italy won comfortably, but in vain, as Croatia triumphed 3–2.

European Championship Record

Formerly part of Yugoslavia. Competing in the European Championship as an independent nation for the first time in 1994–96.

Miroslav Blazevic

Born February 8, 1937. Born at Travnik in Bosnia but of a Croat family, Blazevic played half-back for Sarajevo, Rijeka and Dinamo Zagreb – whom he helped to victory over Leeds United in the final of the 1966–67 Inter-Cities Fairs' Cup. Blazevic coached widely abroad with success at Lausanne, Grasshopper-Club, Sion and Vevey in Switzerland, as well as the national team, then in France with Nantes and in Greece with PAOK. He runs the Croatian national team alongside technical director Tomislav Ivic.

BIG MATCH TEMPERAMENT ***The Croatian team before their October 1995 qualifier against Italy in Split***

> ***"I think national pride is worth more to us than to any other team in the European Championship."***
>
> *DAVOR SUKER, striker, on playing for Croatia, despite the fact that the players are based around Europe.*

CROATIA

Past European Glories

The history of the European Championship dates back to February 5, 1927 – a historic day on which the secretary of the French federation, Henri Delaunay, suggested such a competition to the world governing body, FIFA. It then took a further 27 years before the next step could be taken, enabled by the founding of UEFA in June, 1954. In March the following year Delaunay, his dream now within reach, became secretary of UEFA. Sadly, he died before he could see his vision brought to life on the pitch. But it is in his honour that the trophy in play carries his name. Its success can be gauged by the number of teams entering; 17 in 1959, 49 in 1996.

France 1960

The first European Nations Cup, as it was then known, lasted little more than a year from start to finish. But then, only 17 countries entered. West Germany, Italy and England were among the initial, cautious, absentees.

The Soviet Union made history by staging the first match – beating Hungary by 3–1 in Moscow on September 28, 1958. The historic first goal was scored by left-winger Anatoly Ilyin from Spartak Moscow, after four minutes. In a preliminary round, the Irish Republic lost 2–0, 0–4 to Czechoslovakia to reduce the original entrants to a manageable 16 teams.

The First Tournament

Spain, having eliminated Poland 7–2 on aggregate in the first round, were due to face the Soviet Union in the quarter-final but withdrew from the competition on political grounds. On the field, Yugoslavia rebounded from a 2–1 first leg defeat in Portugal to win the return 5–1, while France, 9–4, and Czechoslovakia, 5–0, had comprehensive aggregate victories over Austria and Romania respectively.

France, appropriately, hosted the first finals. The format became one-off matches with extra time followed by a coin toss, if necessary, to separate the teams. The Soviet Union including legendary goalkeeper Lev Yashin, thrashed Czechoslovakia, 3–0 in Marseille, while hosts France lost a Paris thriller, 5–4 to Yugoslavia.

Soviet Pride

The Final was played in the old Parc des Princes – just like the first European Champions' Cup Final four years earlier. Just before half time, Yugoslavia scored; the goal was credited to Milan Galic although Soviet skipper Igor Netto deflected his strike into the net. The Soviets struck back. Right-wing Slava Metrevelli netted an equalizer early in the second half and centre-forward Viktor Ponedelnik scored the winner in the second period of extra time.

Finals Tournament

Semi-finals

Yugoslavia	5 – 4	France
Soviet Union	3 – 0	Czechoslovakia

Third Place Play-off

Czechoslovakia	2 – 0	France

Final (July 10, Parc des Princes, Paris)

Soviet Union 2 (Metrevelli 49, Ponedelnik 113)
Yugoslavia 1 (Galic 41)
HT: 0–1. 90 min: 1–1. Att: 17,966. Referee: Ellis (England)

Soviet Union: Yashin, Chekheli, Maslenkin, Krutikov, Voinov, Netto, Metrevelli, Ivanov, Ponedelnik, Bubukhin, Meshki.

Yugoslavia: Vidinic, Durkovic, Miladinovic, Jusufi, Zanetic, Perusic, Matus, Jerkovic, Galic, Sekularac, Kostic.

VITAL PUNCH ***The Soviet's Lev Yashin (1) punches clear as Bora Kostic closes in during the 1960 Final***

1960 – 1964

Spain 1964

The Soviet Union were favourites to retain the trophy in 1964. The finals were something of a political triumph for football since, in the 1960 quarter-finals, Spain had withdrawn rather than play the Soviet Union. Now, four years on, Spain not only provided a host's welcome for the Soviet Union but met them in the Final – and beat them.

The qualifying competition was still organized on a direct elimination basis. Scotland and West Germany were among the absentees – Greece withdrew rather than face Albania – while England competed for the first time and were knocked-out immediately. Alf Ramsey's first competitive experience at national team level ended in a 1–1, 2–5 defeat by a French team inspired by veteran Raymond Kopa.

Unlikely Heroes

But the heroes of the qualifying tournament were Luxembourg. The Grand Duchy received a bye in the first round and were drawn against Holland in the next. The Dutch – respecting the importance of the competition – fielded a full-strength team in Amsterdam, but were shocked in a 1–1 draw. In Rotterdam, Holland fielded many Feyenoord players, but a pair of goals from Binder and inspired goalkeeping by Schmitt were enough for Luxembourg's 2–1 victory.

In the quarter-final Luxembourg met Denmark. They drew 2–2 at home and 3–3 away, a result which would have earned qualification in club competition on away goals. But in the Nations Cup a third game was required and Ole Madsen's strike – he netted all six Danish goals in the tie – ended Luxembourg's semi-final dreams.

In other quarter-finals, Spain comfortably beat the Irish Republic, 7–1 on aggregate, and the Soviet Union defeated Sweden. The Soviets had previously beaten a reviving Italy thanks in part to a penalty save by Lev Yashin from the young Sandro Mazzola. Hungary beat France twice to qualify for the finals in Spain.

Reigning Spain

Denmark were well beaten, 3–0, by the Soviet Union in their semi-final in Barcelona. In Madrid, Spain, leaning on the midfield inspiration of Luis Suarez and the right-wing magic of Amancio, defeated Hungary 2–1.

Spain, coached by José Villalonga and also featuring the great Basque goalkeeper José Iribar, took an early lead in the Final in the Estadio Bernabeu through Jesus Pereda. Khusainov struck back for the Soviet Union two minutes later, but a goal from Real Zaragoza centre-forward Marcelino, with seven minutes remaining in normal time, was the signal for Spanish celebrations.

Finals Tournament

Semi-finals

Spain	2 – 1	Hungary (after extra time)
Soviet Union	3 – 0	Denmark

Third Place Play-off

Hungary	3 – 1	Denmark (after extra time)

Final **(June 21, Santiago Bernabeu, Madrid)**

Spain 2 (Pereda 6, Marcelino 83)
Soviet Union 1 (Khusainov 8)
HT: 1–1. Attendance: 125,000. Referee: Holland (England)

Spain: Iribar, Rivilla, Olivella, Calleja, Zoco, Fuste, Amancio, Pereda, Marcelino, Suarez, Lapetra.

Soviet Union: Yashin, Shustikov, Shesternev, Mudrik, Voronin, Aichkin, Chislenko, Ivanov, Ponedelnik, Korneyev, Khusainov.

Italy 1968

In Italy, for the second successive tournament, the hosts ended up as winners. But Italy needed a replay before defeating Yugoslavia – who thus finished runners-up, just as they had done eight years earlier in France.

The dramatic success of the event was reflected in an increased entry. With 31 nations in the tournament, UEFA converted the qualifying competition from the direct elimination system into a mini-league formula. The eight group winners went into two-legged quarter-finals.

Italy earned the right to stage the finals not through seeding but thanks to a qualifying campaign in which a team under the managership of Ferruccio Valcareggi overcame Cyprus, Switzerland and Romania in the group round, then Bulgaria in the quarter-finals.

Tossed Out

The other finalists were experienced Yugoslavia and Soviet Union as well as the World Cup-holders England. Yugoslavia qualified for the quarter-finals at the expense of West Germany and then repeated their 1960 semi-final triumph by beating France. The Soviet Union had a narrow escape in their quarter-final against Hungary, overcoming a 2–0 first leg deficit to win the home game 3–0. England won their group, which comprised two seasons of the Home International Championships, and defeated Spain twice in the quarter-final.

Finals Tournament

Semi-finals

Yugoslavia	1 – 0	England
Italy	0 – 0	Soviet Union

(Italy won toss of a coin after extra time)

Third Place Play-off

England	2 – 0	Soviet Union

Final (June 8, Olimpico, Rome)
Italy 1 (Domenghini 80)
Yugoslavia 1 (Dzajic 38)
HT: 0–1. 90 min: 1–1. Att: 85,000. Referee: Dienst (Swz)

Italy: Zoff, Castano, Burgnich, Guarneri, Facchetti, Ferrini, Juliano, Lodetti, Domenghini, Anastasi, Prati.

Yugoslavia: Pantelic, Fazlagic, Holcer, Paunovic, Damjanovic, Acimovic, Trivic, Pavlovic, Petkovic, Musemic, Dzajic.

Replay (June 10, Olimpico, Rome)
Italy 2 (Riva 12, Anastasi 31)
Yugoslavia 0
HT: 2–0. Att: 50,000. Ref: Ortiz de Mendibil (Spain)

Italy: Zoff, Salvadore, Burgnich, Guarneri, Facchetti, Rosato, De Sisti, Domenghini, Mazzola, Anastasi, Riva.

Yugoslavia: Pantelic, Fazlagic, Paunovic, Holcer, Damjanovic, Acimovic, Trivic, Pavlovic, Hosic, Musemic, Dzajic.

Italy included great figures such as goalkeeper Dino Zoff, left-back Giacinto Facchetti and attackers Pietro Anastasi and Luigi Riva. But they needed the luck of a toss of a coin to earn a place in the Final after their semi against the Soviet Union finished goalless following extra time. The penalty shoot-out had yet to be introduced into top-level competition, and a replay in the semi-final could not be fitted into the schedule.

Magic Dragan

In the other semi-final, Yugoslavia beat England 1–0 in Florence. In this match Alan Mullery became the first player to be sent off while representing England in a senior international. He retaliated to a bad foul by Trivic by kicking the Slav striker and Dragan Dzajic took advantage of the extra player to score a late winner.

Yugoslavia, inspired by the left-wing skills of Dzajic, were favoured to beat Italy in the Final in Rome. Dzajic provided the Slavs with an early lead but Angelo Domenghini equalized controversially from a free kick with 10 minutes remaining. Extra-time failed to provide any more goals so the Final went to a replay. This time Yugoslavia were too tired to resist the thrusts of Riva and Anastasi. Italy were European champions for the first – and, so far, only – time.

Happy captain ***Italy's Giacinto Facchetti parades the Henri Delaunay Cup after the Final replay***

CELEBRATION TIME *German fans invade the Heysel Stadium pitch after their team's Final victory*

Belgium 1972

West Germany had thrilled World Cup followers in 1970 in a 4–3 semi-final defeat by Italy. But manager Helmut Schön created almost a new team for the European Championship – and a team which proved even more spectacular.

The nucleus of the team was provided by the top German clubs of the time, Bayern Munich and Borussia Moenchengladbach. The creative combination of Bayern's revolutionary attacking sweeper, Franz Beckenbauer, and Borussia's playmaker Gunter Netzer, lit up the European game. The assistance of adventurous young left-back Paul Breitner and supreme marksman Gerd Müller left no doubt that the right team had earned the crown of European champions.

DRAWING ON EXPERIENCE

The format for the tournament was the same as four years earlier. This time, West Germany overran England – who had the best record of the eight quarter-finalists – 3–1 at Wembley and drew 0–0 in Berlin.

In the other quarter-finals, the Soviet Union won a repeat of the 1960 Final against Yugoslavia, winning 3–0 at home after drawing the first leg. The other two quarter-finals also were level after the first matches. Belgium defeated the holders Italy 2–1 in their second game, but Hungary and Romania drew a second time before the former won a playoff, 2–1.

The finals were staged in Belgium. In Antwerp, West Germany overcame the hosts 2–1, while in Brussels, the Soviet Union continued their very consistent record in this competition by beating Hungary 1–0 in their semi-final. It was the Soviet Union's third final in four tournaments, a record which could have been perfect had the coin toss in Italy gone the other way after their draw with the hosts. In one respect the record was perfect; the Soviets did not concede a goal in any of their four semi-final appearances.

GERMAN SUPREMACY

The Soviet Union team was completely changed from the sides which had contested the finals in 1960 and 1964. Although the old guard, most notably the great goalkeeper Lev Yashin, had retired, the defence with Rudakov in goal remained solid and had conceded only one goal in their last six championship matches.

But Beckenbauer and his team were clear favourites to win the Final in the Heysel stadium in Brussels. The Soviet Union never threatened. Netzer dominated midfield and hit a post before two typically opportunist strikes from Müller and another from Herbert Wimmer decided the match. The 3–0 scoreline remains the largest winning margin of any European Championship final.

Finals Tournament

SEMI-FINALS

Soviet Union	1 – 0	Hungary
West Germany	2 – 1	Belgium

THIRD PLACE PLAY-OFF

Belgium	2 – 1	Hungary

FINAL (JUNE 18, HEYSEL, BRUSSELS)
West Germany 3 (Müller 27, 57, Wimmer 52)
Soviet Union 0
HT: 1–0. Att: 50,000. Ref: Marschall (Austria)

West Germany: Maier, Hottges, Beckenbauer, Schwarzenbeck, Breitner, Hoeness, Netzer, Wimmer, Heynckes, G Muller, E Kremers.

Soviet Union: Rudakov, Dzodzuashvili, Khurtsilava, Kaplichny, Istomin, Kolotov, Troshkin, Konkov (Dolmatov 46), Baidachny, Banishevski (Kozenkevich 65), Onishenko.

Yugoslavia 1976

If the 1972 European Championship finals had produced an outstanding team in West Germany, the 1976 event went three better by producing four superbly competitive sides. Hosts – and two-time finalists – Yugoslavia finished fourth after losing the third place play-off to Holland, but there could be no disgrace or embarrassment in that. These stand as probably the most thrilling finals of the "first" generation of the tournament – with the Final between Czechoslovakia and holders West Germany a dramatic classic.

Once again the formula provided for a first round of mini-leagues followed by direct elimination quarter-finals and then the finals themselves. The only change in the competition's format was that, in the knock-out stages, penalty kicks would decide drawn matches after extra time.

Czechoslovakia, under the expert guidance of Vaclav Jezek, defeated the favoured Soviet Union 2–0 and 2–2 in the quarter-finals. Holland, World Cup runners-up two years earlier and inspired by Johan Cruyff and Johan Neeskens, defeated neighbours Belgium. West Germany, now also the world as well as European champions, overran Spain and Yugoslavia won a bad-tempered tie with Wales to earn both a semi-final place and host rights. This was the first and – so far – last time that the finals had been staged in eastern Europe.

90 Minutes Not Enough

The pattern of excitement was set when Czechoslovakia defeated Holland 3–1 after extra time in the first semi-final – the Dutch succumbing after the Welsh referee Clive Thomas had sent off two Dutchmen, Neeskens and Wim Van Hanegem. Then it was West Germany's turn to need extra time as they hit back from 2–0 down to beat hosts Yugoslavia 4–2.

The Germans had found a new Müller – Dieter Müller from Köln. He scored a hat-trick against Yugoslavia and led the German fightback in the Final in Belgrade after they had gone 2–0 down in 25 minutes to Czechoslovakia. One minute remained in normal time when Bernd Holzenbein's headed equalizer from Rainer Bonhof's corner sent the game into extra-time.

Spot On

No goals came in the extra period and Czechoslovakia duly won the first major event decided on a penalty shoot-out. Czechoslovakia went first and scored. In fact, the first seven were all converted. But with number eight, Uli Hoeness blasted his attempt high and wide, so when midfield general Antonin Panenka sent goalkeeper Sepp Maier the wrong way with the ninth kick there could be no German comeback.

Finals Tournament

Semi-finals

Czechoslovakia	3 – 1	Holland (after extra time)
West Germany	4 – 2	Yugoslavia (after extra time)

Third Place Play-off

Holland	3 – 2	Yugoslavia (after extra time)

Final (June 20, Marakana, Belgrade)

Czechoslovakia 2 (Svehlik 8, Dobias 25)
West Germany 2 (D Müller 28, Holzenbein 89)
HT: 2–1. 90 min: 2–2. Att: 33,000. Ref: Gonella (Italy)
Czechoslovakia won 5–3 on penalties after extra time

Czechoslovakia: Viktor, Pivarnik, Ondrus, Capkovic, Gogh, Dobias (F Vesely), Panenka, Moder, Masny, Svehlik (Jurkemik 79), Nehoda.

West Germany: Maier, Vogts, Beckenbauer, Schwarzenbeck, Dietz, Wimmer (Flohe 46), Bonhof, Beer (Bongartz 79), Hoeness, D Müller, Holzenbein.

ONE MORE EFFORT ***Czechoslovak coach Vaclav Jezek prepares his players for extra-time in the Final***

Turning point ***Karl-Heinz Rummenigge outpaces Belgium's Luc Millecamps in the Stadio Olimpico***

Italy 1980

The European Championship entered a new era. Such was the popularity of the tournament and the pressure for places in the finals, that UEFA decided to increase the scope of the finals to take in eight countries – split into two groups of four with the group winners meeting in the Final.

Italy became the first nation to host the finals twice – they also earned automatic qualification – and were matched in their group with England, Belgium and Spain. The other group featured old rivals West Germany and Holland, title-holders Czechoslovakia and newcomers Greece, who qualified ahead of the Soviet Union, Hungary and Finland with only seven points from six games.

Goals at a Premium

On the pitch the group format was criticized because 12 games produced only 22 goals. That, however, certainly did not reduce the passion among the crowds – particularly in Turin where riot police unleashed tear gas to quell unrest among supporters during England's opening draw against Belgium in the old Stadio Comunale.

Belgium beat Spain 2–1 in their next game but England's dreams of a place in the Final in Rome disintegrated as they lost 1–0 to their hosts. Juventus midfielder Marco Tardelli scored the winner 10 minutes from the end. A goalless draw with Italy on the last matchday was enough to send Belgium into their first major final.

West Germany, quickly establishing themselves as event favourites, topped the other group. They began with a 1–0 revenge victory over Czechoslovakia, followed up with a 3–2 win over Holland in Naples – in which the TV-watching world "discovered" the inspirational midfielder Bernd Schuster – and played out a goalless draw with Greece.

Roman Anticlimax

The German hero, now that Gerd Müller and Franz Beckenbauer had moved on, was another Bayern Munich player, Karl-Heinz Rummenigge. He justified his reputation in the Final against Belgium in Rome. After Vandereycken's second half penalty had cancelled out Horst Hrubesch's early strike, Rummenigge delivered the inch-perfect corner which the giant Hrubesch headed for the last-minute winner.

A 48,000 crowd, well below capacity, turned out. It would have been different if Italy had been playing but they fell to Czechoslovakia in the third place play-off the previous evening in Naples. A lacklustre game reached its nadir in a penalty shoot-out which the Czechoslovaks eventually won, 9–8. The lesson was quickly learned and the third place play-off – always an anti-climax, even for the two teams involved – was scrapped.

Finals Tournament

Group 1

West Germany	1 – 0	Czechoslovakia
Holland	1 – 0	Greece
West Germany	3 – 2	Holland
Czechoslovakia	3 – 1	Greece
Czechoslovakia	1 – 1	Holland
West Germany	0 – 0	Greece

Table

	P	W	D	L	F	A	Pts
West Germany	3	2	1	0	4	2	5
Czechoslovakia	3	1	1	1	4	3	3
Holland	3	1	1	1	4	4	3
Greece	3	0	1	2	2	4	1

Group 2

England	1 – 1	Belgium
Italy	0 – 0	Spain
Belgium	2 – 1	Spain
Italy	1 – 0	England
England	2 – 1	Spain
Italy	0 – 0	Belgium

Table

	P	W	D	L	F	A	Pts
Belgium	3	1	2	0	3	2	4
Italy	3	1	2	0	1	0	4
England	3	1	1	1	3	3	3
Spain	3	0	1	2	2	4	1

Third Place Play-off

Czechoslovakia 1 – 1 Italy
(Czechoslovakia 9–8 on penalties after extra time)

Final (June 22, Olimpico, Rome)

West Germany 2 (Hrubesch 10, 88)
Belgium 1 (Vandereycken 71, pen)
HT: 1–0. Att: 48,000. Ref: Rainea (Rom)

West Germany: Schumacher, Kaltz, Stielike, KH Forster, Dietz, Briegel (Cullmann 55), Schuster, H Müller, KH Rummenigge, Hrubesch, K Allofs.

Belgium: Pfaff, Gerets, L Millecamps, Meeuws, Renquin, Cools, Vandereycken, Van Moer, Mommens, François Van der Elst, Ceulemans.

COSTLY SLIP ***Michel Platini's shot squeezes through Luis Arconada's hands for France's opening goal***

France 1984

Most nations' victories in events occasionally raise the eyebrow of controversy and critical suggestions that success would have been beyond them in another country. Such criticism could never have been levelled against the magnificent French side who swept all before them to win the ultimate prize in the new Parc des Princes in Paris.

The changing balance of the international game was reflected in the make-up of the finals. France, increasingly impressive at international level over the previous six years, were not merely the best national team in Europe but also the most skilled and entertaining. Their brilliance emanated from the midfield trio of hard-working Luis Fernandez and Jean Tigana plus effervescent little Alain Giresse – all topped off by the all-round attacking genius of Michel Platini.

There was yet another change to the format, but this was a small one, allowing for semi-finals.

ABSENT FRIENDS

The presence of Denmark's rising force in the finals was another gesture towards a new balance of power within Europe, as was the failure of West Germany to reach the semi-finals.

Led by Allan Simonsen – a former European Footballer of the Year, Denmark qualified at England's expense, but the most dramatic qualifying group involved Spain and Holland. Entering the final match, Spain needed to beat Malta by 11 goals to qualify; they missed a penalty but still won 12–1! Both the score and the margin of victory are records for the European Championship. Spain went to the finals because they scored two more goals than Holland – 24 to 22 – though both had the same goal difference.

VIVE LA FRANCE

Denmark were one of the favourites, but injury wrecked their prospects in the finals – Simonsen suffered a broken leg – which they opened with a 1–0 defeat by France. Platini was the match-winner, scoring the first of his nine goals in five games. His haul included hat-tricks against Belgium and Yugoslavia, a last-minute semi-final winner in extra-time against Portugal, and the first goal of the Final itself against Spain.

Injuries and suspensions during the tournament ruined Spain's tactical plan, but it was an uncharacteristic slip by goalkeeper-captain Luis Arconada, allowing Platini's low drive from a free kick to spin through his grasp, which proved the decisive blow after 56 minutes. Bruno Bellone scored the second for France in the last minute but their lead, despite Le Roux's late sending-off, had never been seriously threatened.

Finals Tournament

GROUP 1

France	1 – 0	Denmark
Belgium	2 – 0	Yugoslavia
France	5 – 0	Belgium
Denmark	5 – 0	Yugoslavia
France	3 – 2	Yugoslavia
Denmark	3 – 2	Belgium

TABLE

	P	W	D	L	F	A	Pts
France	3	3	0	0	9	2	6
Denmark	3	2	0	1	8	3	4
Belgium	3	1	0	2	4	8	2
Yugoslavia	3	0	0	3	2	10	0

GROUP 2

West Germany	0 – 0	Portugal
Spain	1 – 1	Romania
West Germany	2 – 1	Romania
Portugal	1 – 1	Spain
Spain	1 – 0	West Germany
Portugal	1 – 0	Romania

TABLE

	P	W	D	L	F	A	Pts
Spain	3	1	2	0	3	2	4
Portugal	3	1	2	0	2	1	4
West Germany	3	1	1	1	2	2	3
Romania	3	0	1	2	2	4	1

SEMI-FINALS

France	3 – 2	Portugal
Spain	1 – 1	Denmark

(Spain 5–4 on penalties after extra time)

FINAL (JUNE 27, PARC DES PRINCES, PARIS)

France 2 (Platini 56, Bellone 90) Spain 0
HT: 0–0. Att: 47,368. Ref: Christov (Czechoslovakia)

France: Bats, Battiston (Amoros 72), Le Roux, Bossis, Domergue, Fernandez, Giresse, Tigana, Platini, Lacombe (Genghini 79), Bellone.
Le Roux sent off, 84 min.

Spain: Arconada, Urquiaga, Salva (Roberto 84), Gallego, Senor, Francisco, Victor, Camacho, Julio Alberto (Sarabia 76), Santillana, Carrasco.

West Germany 1988

Holland, runners-up in the World Cups of both 1974 and 1978, finally secured the major prize for which their pre-eminence in the international game had long since earned. They were the best team throughout the tournament.

Victory made a nonsense of fears that the generation which produced Johan Cruyff, Rob Rensenbrink, Johan Neeskens and Co had been a mere slip in time. Holland's victory over the Soviet Union in the 1988 Final in Munich's Olympic stadium was serious evidence in favour of the Dutch approach to youth coaching and to all aspects of general football intelligence.

For once, the format was unchanged. A qualifying section of seven mini-leagues – with the hosts exempt – was climaxed by two groups of four teams each in the finals, followed by semi-finals and final.

Irish Eyes are Smiling

England arrived in West Germany for the finals with the best record of any of the qualifiers, winning five and drawing their other match, scoring 19 goals and conceding just one. Their form then deserted them – starting with a 1–0 set-back against the Irish Republic newcomers and continuing with a comprehensive defeats by Holland – for whom Marco Van Basten scored a scintillating hat-trick – and the Soviet Union.

Van Basten had been uncertain of his place at the start of the finals. It was his friend and mentor Johan Cruyff who persuade him to stay with the squad. When Van Basten was substituted towards the end of the England game, he shook hands with coach Rinus Michels as he left the pitch. That handshake came to symbolize the new-found unity of spirit which carried Holland to victory.

Dutch Masters

West Germany topped the other group without appearing convincing but they led Holland in their semi-final in Hamburg thanks to a Lothar Matthäus penalty after a foul on Jürgen Klinsmann. Holland hit back immediately when Ronald Koeman fired home a penalty of their own and Van Basten snatched a late winner.

Finals Tournament

Group 1

West Germany	1 – 1	Italy
Spain	3 – 2	Denmark
West Germany	2 – 0	Denmark
Italy	1 – 0	Spain
West Germany	2 – 0	Spain
Italy	2 – 0	Denmark

Table

	P	W	D	L	F	A	Pts
West Germany	3	2	1	0	5	1	5
Italy	3	2	1	0	4	1	5
Spain	3	1	0	2	3	5	2
Denmark	3	0	0	3	2	7	0

Group 2

Republic of Ireland	1 – 0	England
Soviet Union	1 – 0	Holland
Holland	3 – 1	England
Republic of Ireland	1 – 1	Soviet Union
Soviet Union	3 – 1	England
Holland	1 – 0	Republic of Ireland

Table

	P	W	D	L	F	A	Pts
Soviet Union	3	2	1	0	5	2	5
Holland	3	2	0	1	4	2	4
Republic of Ireland	3	1	1	1	2	2	3
England	3	0	0	3	2	7	0

Semi-finals

Holland	2 – 1	West Germany
Soviet Union	2 – 0	Italy

Final (June 25, Olympiastadion, Munich)

Holland 2 (Gullit 33, Van Basten 54)
Soviet Union 0
HT: 1–0. Att: 72,300. Ref: Vautrot (France)

Holland: Van Breukelen, Van Aerle, R Koeman, Rijkaard, Van Tiggelen, Vanenburg, Wouters, E Koeman, Muhren, Gullit, Van Basten.

Soviet Union: Dasayev, Khidiatulin, Demianenko, Litovchenko, Aleinikov, Zavarov, Mikhailichenko, Gotsmanov (Baltacha 69), Rats, Belanov, Protasov (Pasulko 71).

In the Final, Holland met a Soviet side which was missing the significant defensive presence of Oleg Kuznetsov through suspension. Not even Kuznetsov, however, would have been able to control the attacking flair of Van Basten and skipper Ruud Gullit in the Dutch attack. Gullit scored the first goal and Van Basten the second – volleying home one of the greatest individual goals ever seen in any major international event. The Soviet Union's final chance was a 57th minute penalty, but Hans Van Breukelen – who needlessly brought down Igor Belanov – saved the same player's kick.

RUUD AWAKENING ***Holland's Ruud Gullit was one of the stars of the 1988 tournament***

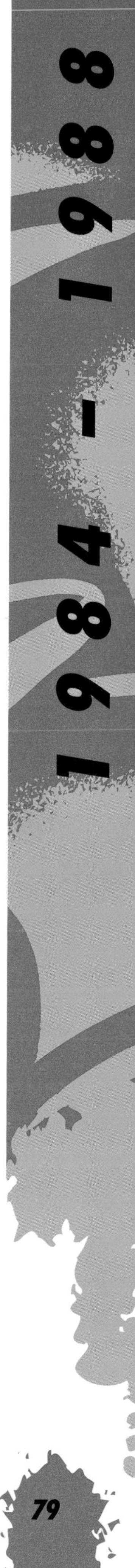

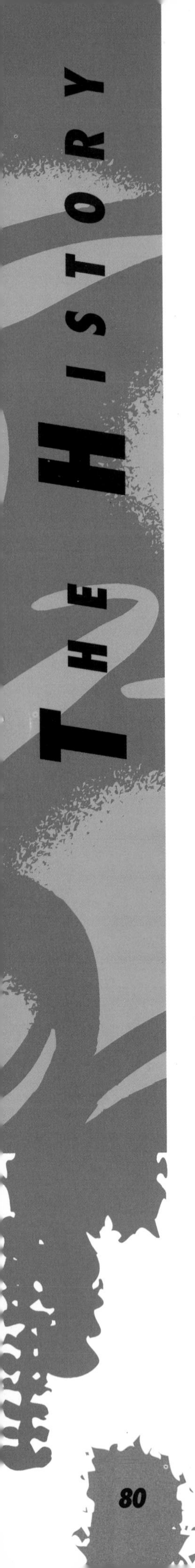

Sweden 1992

The story of the 1992 finals was straight out of a Hans Christian Andersen fairytale. Denmark came from nowhere to win the tournament for the first time in their history and overcame more fancied opponents, first Holland in the semi-final and then Germany in the Final, to do so.

Sweden was the peaceful venue for the climax of this championship, which had been shaken to its roots by political upheavals almost from the very start – and which saw the Soviet Union transformed into the ponderous Commonwealth of Independent States between the start of the qualifying competition and the finals.

Two into One

Elsewhere, the former East Germany was consigned to political history just as the qualifying tournament began and the GDR federation, as one of its last acts, pulled out of the qualifiers, allowing key players, such as midfielder Matthias Sammer and forwards Thomas Doll and Andreas Thom, to appear for a unified Germany in the finals.

Then there was Yugoslavia. They had been one of the most outstanding of the qualifiers. But the spring of 1992 saw the onset of the country's violent collapse. In the wake of United Nations sanctions, UEFA barred them from the finals, citing security grounds, and recalled Denmark – the Slavs' qualifying group runners-up – in their stead. Denmark had just two weeks' notice of their place in Sweden.

On a positive note, France had become the first nation ever to qualify for the finals by winning every group game.

Fairytale Ending

Hosts Sweden, in the finals for the first time, deservedly topped Group A. A wonderful goal by Tomas Brolin brought Sweden a place at the top of the group and a 2–1 victory over a disappointing England in the final group match. By beating a similarly lacklustre French team, Denmark followed Sweden into the semi-finals.

In Group B, Holland and Germany possessed too much firepower and experience for newcomers Scotland and the CIS. Holland then threw it away against Denmark in the semi-final, being held 2–2 and losing 5–4 on penalties. The vital penalty miss came from Marco Van Basten, the hero four years earlier. Brolin scored again for Sweden in their semi-final, but in vain as West Germany won 3–2.

Berti Vogts's men were clear favourites in the Final. But Denmark – from manager Richard Moller Nielsen through goalkeeper Peter Schmeichel, skipper Lars Olsen, midfielder Kim Vilfort and forward Brian Laudrup – had not read the script. Goals from John Jensen and Vilfort duly produced the greatest shock in the competition's history.

Finals Tournament

Group A

Sweden	1 – 1	France
Denmark	0 – 0	England
France	0 – 0	England
Sweden	1 – 0	Denmark
Denmark	2 – 1	France
Sweden	2 – 1	England

Table

	P	W	D	L	F	A	Pts
Sweden	3	2	1	0	4	2	5
Denmark	3	1	1	1	2	2	3
France	3	0	2	1	2	3	2
England	3	0	2	1	1	2	2

Group B

Holland	1 – 0	Scotland
Germany	1 – 1	CIS
Germany	2 – 0	Scotland
Holland	0 – 0	CIS
Holland	3 – 1	Germany
Scotland	3 – 0	CIS

Table

	P	W	D	L	F	A	Pts
Holland	3	2	1	0	4	1	5
Germany	3	1	1	1	2	2	3
Scotland	3	1	0	2	3	3	2
CIS	3	0	2	1	1	4	2

Semi-finals

Germany	3 – 2	Sweden
Denmark	2 – 2	Holland

(Denmark 5–4 on penalties after extra time)

Final (June 26, Nya Ullevi, Gothenburg)

Denmark 2 (Jensen 18, Vilfort 78)
Germany 0
HT: 1–0. Att: 37,800. Ref: Galler (Switzerland)

Denmark: Schmeichel, Sivebaek (Christiansen 66), K Nielsen, L Olsen, Piechnik, Christofte, Vilfort, J Jensen, H Larsen, B Laudrup, Povlsen.

Germany: Illgner, Reuter, Kohler, Helmer, Brehme, Buchwald, Effenberg (Thom 80), Sammer (Doll 46), Hassler, Klinsmann, Riedle.

THEY ALL LIVED HAPPILY EVER AFTER ***Denmark's fairy-tale Championship ended with victory in the Final***